web sites
made
painless

THIS IS A CARLTON BOOK

Text and design copyright © Carlton Books 2000

A CIP Catalogue for this book is available from the British Library

ISBN 1 85868 955 4

Project Editor: Lara Maiklem
Production: Sarah Corteel

Created by Gecko Grafx Ltd

Notice of Liability
Every effort has been made to ensure that this book contains accurate and current information. However, the Publisher and the author shall not be liable for any loss or damage suffered by the readers as a result of any information contained herein.

Trademarks
Macromedia, the Macromedia logo, Fireworks, Flash and Dreamweaver are trademarks or registered trademarks of Macromedia Inc.
All other trademarks are acknowledged as belonging to their respective companies

Printed and bound in Italy

web sites
made
painless

Christophe Dillinger

CARLTON BOOKS

CONTENTS

GETTING STARTED

1

The company you work for has one. Your gym has one too and so does your supermarket. The shops where you buy your CDs and books have one. There's even a good chance that your neighbour has one. So it's probably about time you got yourself one too, isn't it? As little as three years ago, designing and building a web site was difficult and time-consuming. Now, with a wide variety of web design software packages available it can be quick and easy.

WHAT IS A WEB SITE?

Before we start, we will assume you can operate a computer and that you are familiar with things like cutting and pasting text and pictures, creating folders and saving, renaming and retrieving files. We will also assume that you don't know anything about creating web sites. When you finish reading this book and following the instructions, you will. You'll begin to wonder what all the fuss was about.

A WEB SITE?

The best thing to compare a web site to is probably a book. Like a book, a web site is made up of a number of pages. Those pages can contain text, images, tables and graphs, a table of contents… You make your way around a book by turning the pages: with a web site, you navigate by clicking on hyperlinks and jumping to them. Books sometimes make reference to other books. Web sites make reference to other pages and to other sites, and that's just the start of the differences. When you navigate a site, you can link straight to another site, not just mention it. Some books (especially those for children) can contain sounds. They can't contain animations or movie clips, though. You can't write to the author of the book and say that you liked it (or hated it!) a lot from within the pages. You can with a web site. You can also set a site up so that you know how many people have read your pages, what time they read them, what kind of computer they have, how long they stayed… and unlike a book, a web page can be read by millions of people simultaneously – no one has to look over anyone else's shoulder.

WHAT DO THEY DO?

A web site is a window from you to the rest of the world. It can show what your hobbies are, what you like and dislike, what you think, what you sell … Web sites are not only for big corporate companies; they are for absolutely everybody. They are a way of communicating and sharing information with millions of other web users and getting near-instantaneous feedback from people all over the world. The chances are that if you need information about the preparation of artichokes in the 18th century in Southern Asia, somebody has written a web page about it. The Web boasted, in the early months of the year 2000, over one billion documents and over 120 million users. You are pretty much guaranteed to find what you are looking for (eventually) and one of the joys is that there is certainly enough room for you to contribute to this awesome mass of information, on a business or personal level, or both.

HTML

Web pages are written in a special type of computer code called HTML, which stands for HyperText Markup Language. HTML is a set of instructions called "tags" that can be translated and displayed by any web browser (the program you will use to view web sites).

HTML code tells the web browser where to place a picture in the page currently viewed, where this picture file really is, what colour the text for the caption should be, how big the text should be, what font it should be in, and so on. HTML is an industry recognized standard, so all web browsers are built to support it.

The most common web browsers are Microsoft's Internet Explorer and Netscape's Navigator.

This is what HTML code looks like when it is written.

```
<body bgcolor="white" onload="MM_preloadImages('images/profile.gif','#
    <table cool width="163" height="438" border="0" cellpadding="0" ce
        <tr height="1" cntrlrow>
            <td width="1" height="1"></td>
            <td width="160" height="1"><spacer type="block" width="160
        </tr>
```

Fortunately, you don't need to learn HTML any more. Time was when you had to learn this "language" to be able to put your information on the Internet. Although a computer language, HTML is actually quite easy to learn and requires no programming skills. These days, web design programs such as Macromedias's Dreamweaver or Microsoft's FrontPage will take care of everything for you and generate HTML code from your layouts. If you really want to learn HTML, you can write it using a simple, no-frills text editor like Microsoft Wordpad or SimpleText.

Because the Web is a medium that is constantly evolving, HTML changes all the time and gets "polluted" with more powerful scripting languages ("proper" programming languages) such as JAVA, JAVAScript, CGI, ASP and PERL. You will not have to learn these either, though. These languages enable web pages to display more information and to interact faster and better with the viewer. They are mostly behind the rise of e-commerce. Luckily, most of the codes for these languages that you will need have already been written, so you can just use existing codes for your web sites, if you need to.

WWW

You have probably seen these three letters before, on posters, business cards or CDs, and you will have heard them spelled out on the radio or on TV. But what actually is the World Wide Web? When you link two computers together, you have a network. Add more computers and you have an intranet (as for a small office). When this network can be accessed from the outside via a telephone line, it becomes the Internet. The Web (short for World Wide Web) is the mother of all networks, linking all the available networks together in one huge system that can be accessed from anywhere at any time by anybody.

After research by the military into keeping communication channels open following nuclear war, the first vestiges of the Internet were set up by American universities so that they could share data (originally just two computers networked together in the early 1970s). With the stunning rise of home computer use, the Internet metamorphosed itself into the Web.

Mosaic, one of the original web browsers, is still going strong.

America On-Line is one of the biggest Internet Service Providers in the world. Its merge with Time-Warner in January 2000 heralded a new era of multimedia power.

THE FUTURE OF THE WEB

As its name suggests, the Web is a world-wide phenomenon. It has broken the barriers between countries and led the way towards a generalization and globalization of communication, and more to the point for its survival, commerce. Information is near-instantaneous and can be shared by anyone having the resources to hook themselves up to a news server. It is forecasted that more and more services will be available online and that shopping on the Web will become a part of our way of life. Because of its incredible rate of growth, the Web has created hundreds of thousands of new jobs and boosted computer technology.

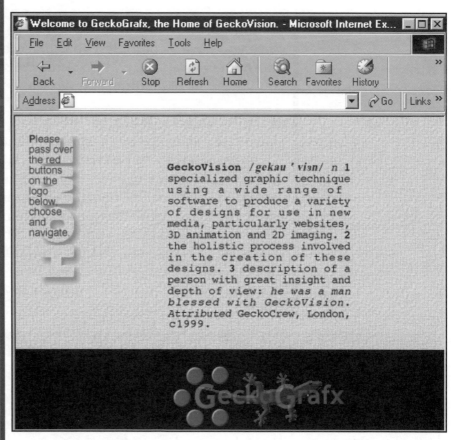

A typical commercial web site.

SETTING UP

There are a few things you will need to build your web site. One of them is a computer: a web site is a 100 per cent digital adventure and cannot be built without one.

Building your own web site need not be an expensive affair. Once you have a computer, you can access a lot of online information, graphics and free programs to help you. What you'll need most are time and dedication.

REQUIREMENTS: HARDWARE

Hardware means the bits and pieces that make a computer. Your computer doesn't have to be the latest powerhouse or supercomputer; any computer will do, but remember that the more powerful your system, the easier and faster your work is going to be. You will also need a modem. It is the piece of equipment that connects you to the internet (the term modem stands for MODulator-DEModulator). Once again, the faster the better (and cheaper in the long term too as you'll spend less time online). Along with a modem you'll need a phone line to connect to the Web. A scanner can help if you want to

TYPICAL SETUP   ▫ ⬒ ✕

A typical setup would be a computer with at least a 300 MHz CPU and 64 Megabytes of memory, although more would enable you to run more programs at the same time without any strain on your system. Your modem should be a 56K one at least. It can be either internal (plugged inside your computer) or external. You should have a 15 inch (35cm) monitor, although the extra room of a 17 inch (40cm) one makes quite a lot of difference to the way you can work.

add your own personalized images to your site. A digital camera and a graphics tablet can prove useful too but are luxuries for most people.

REQUIREMENTS: SOFTWARE

In this book, most examples will come from Dreamweaver 3.0, a web design program released by Macromedia, but we'll also look at other packages. Dreamweaver is relatively cheap and very easy to use. You don't need this particular program to publish on the Web, though; any web design software will do. Check out the free demonstration software from computer magazine cover disks, try them out and then choose the one that suits you best. Other popular packages include Adobe GoLive 4.0, Microsoft FrontPage and a heap of shareware programs that can do the job just as nicely.

Strictly speaking, you don't even need a web design program to build your homepage: a simple text editor such as Notepad for Windows will do the trick. But this is the painful way of doing things, requiring you to remember HTML code, syntax and various rules, and this book has been put together to make matters painless.

Dreamweaver from Macromedia is just one of many web site design packages.

WEB BROWSERS

A web browser is the software that you use to navigate sites on the web. The most popular ones are Internet Explorer (IE) and Netscape Navigator, both available for nothing. An important note: try to get the latest version of these web browsers. The web is a rapidly moving medium and you do need to try to keep up with technology. You will need at least one of these browsers (although both would be an advantage) to check what the end product looks like before publishing it.

You will also need some sort of graphic manipulation package. You will need to edit images, reduce their size and save them in proper web-friendly formats, such as GIF or JPEG (more on these later). Many people use Adobe Photoshop, but it can be a bit expensive if all you need is to modify a few images, so you might wish to go for PaintShop Pro, or any image-processing freeware.

INTERNET CONNECTION

You connect to the web via an ISP (an Internet Service Provider). There are plenty of ISPs available for free; all you need to do is to check – once again – computer magazine cover disks. ISPs usually offer what is called web space (usually from 10 to 50 megabytes), which is a folder created by your ISP on one of their hard disks on their web servers. This is the place where your site will be stored and accessed. Some free ISPs will modify your pages so that each time someone views them, a commercial message will be displayed (either in another window or as a logo on your pages). This is fine if your site isn't going to be a professional or a commercial one. If it is, you might wish to pay for an ISP. Always shop around for a good deal or ask other people to work out who seems like a good bet.

There are, finally, a lot of other programs available that can make your life easier when you are building your site: graphic animation programs, sound editors, plugins… They are certainly not vital for web designing, but they can help, especially when you get a bit more adventurous. More will be said about these later (see Chapter 8). Computer magazines

QuickTime™

Some specific file formats will need a "plugin" to run in a web browser. A plugin is a piece of software that runs in your browser to display special "objects" like movies or special sounds. QuickTime and Macromedia Flash are two popular examples.

often offer free graphics, clip art and animated images to liven up your pages too.

ON YOUR DRIVES

Getting organized is one of the keys to successful, stress-free web site building. To start with, you will need a folder somewhere on your hard disk where you will store your pages, your images, your movies – in short, all the various elements that will appear in your site. We'll call this your "root" folder. Then you will need a folder for each separate section of your site. A typical setup would contain at least a folder called "images". Another useful folder would be a "work in progress" folder, created outside your root folder, to store all your first drafts and your working images and pages.

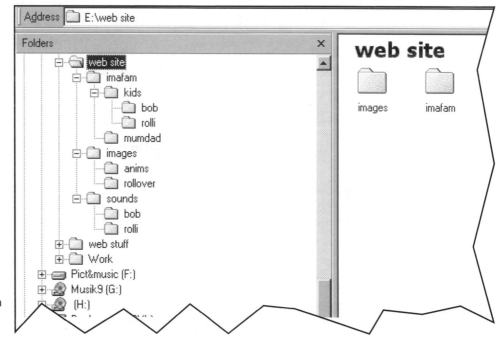

Things can get complicated very quickly so a tidy setup can really help.

This setup is by no mean extensive. Try to arrange your folders according to the content of your site. Nothing stops you from creating a "french" folder for the French versions of your pages if you have one and then an "image" folder inside it if you need to display specifically French pictures.

PLANNING AHEAD

Make sure your machine is in proper working order before you start. Then, think for a while about what you want your site to look like, what you want in it and what you are trying to say. It is usually a good idea to draw a rough draft of the general layout of your site rather than just try to put it together without a concrete idea in your head. As you would for a book or a story, try to write a plan with chapters and a table of contents for your site. Picture in your head – and then on paper – where everything will go and have all the images and text ready before you start. You can always change your plans when you've begun.

Organizing your work will help you a lot in keeping track of what is going on with your site, especially if you think of more material to add as you go along. Make sure that all the relevant pictures are stored in the same relevant folder. The same goes for your web files (your HTML files), your movie clips, your sound files and your drafts.

COPYRIGHT

If you plan on using copyrighted material (i.e. something that you didn't create yourself), make sure that you have the author's permission to do so: scanning a page from a magazine and publishing it on the Web without written consent from the magazine's editor is illegal and asking for trouble. If you are in doubt about what is copyrighted or not, don't publish it unless you have written permission to do so, not just an email from someone you think is probably the owner.

MATERIAL SOURCES

The content of your web pages can come from various sources. Almost any document, image, sound or text that can be transformed into a computer file of some sort can be placed on a web page.

When you have your site planned and once all the information, documents and resources have been collected or created and are all stored in their relevant folders, it is safe to run your software and start putting the puzzle together.

Links to another page another member of the family has created.

Your own artwork created from scratch using a graphic package.

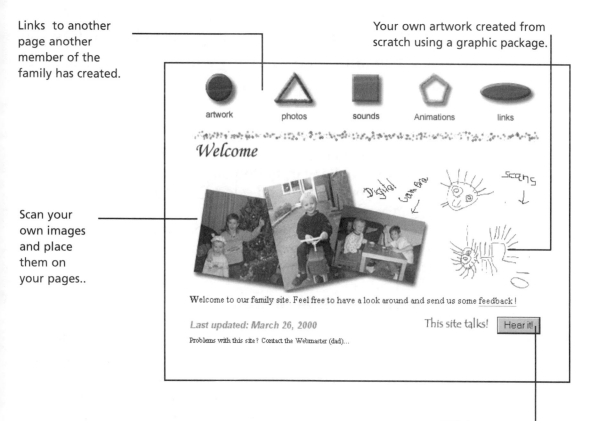

Scan your own images and place them on your pages..

A link to a page full of sounds.

We live in the digital age and virtually anything that is stored on a computer can be inserted into a web page.

REAMWEAVER

The most popular web design program at the moment is Dreamweaver, released by Macromedia. It is relatively cheap and very versatile in the sense that it can be as simple or as complex as you wish it to be. You can use it to start learning web site-building the easy way and then carry on with more complicated actions later, when you feel more confident.

First install Dreamweaver 3 from your CD, choosing Typical Install. When this is done, you will be able to run the program by clicking on the Start button on your taskbar (the bar at the bottom of your screen) and select Programs/Macromedia Dreamweaver 3/Dreamweaver 3.

Dreamweaver 3's interface (the collection of toolbars and menus) is clear and everything you need is accessible at the click of a button.

ARRANGING YOUR MENUS

Every time you start a new document, it will appear in its own window, with its own menu bar at the top. Click on Windows in it to get a list of all the toolbars available to you and arrange them on your desktop: Dreamweaver 3 will remember their position and they will be available where you left them the next time you run it. Dreamweaver 3 is a WYSIWYG programme, which stands for What You See Is What You Get. All this means is that the way you position your text, images and effects will, in theory, reflect what you will get in your web browser when you have finished.

The <u>Objects</u> palette. This contains buttons that you will use to place text, pictures and other objects

<u>Launcher</u>. The buttons in this palette are used to open and close other palettes

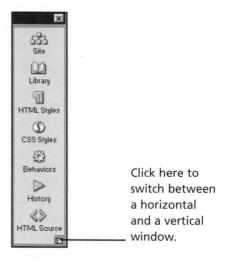

Click here to switch between a horizontal and a vertical window.

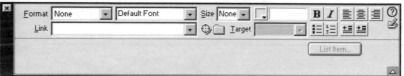

The <u>Properties Inspector</u>. You will use this to examine and change the properties of objects in your document. Click the arrow in the bottom right corner to extend the full window and access the advanced options.

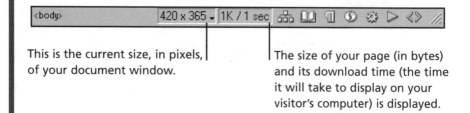

This is the current size, in pixels, of your document window.

The size of your page (in bytes) and its download time (the time it will take to display on your visitor's computer) is displayed.

At the bottom of your blank document is a row of icons – the same as on the <u>Launcher</u> toolbar – called the <u>Mini Launcher</u>. If you do not have much space on your screen, you can turn the <u>Launcher</u> palette off by clicking on the cross icon in the top right corner of it.

As for virtually all Windows programs, you can access advanced settings and various options by right-clicking on an item in a window, such as an image or some text. These menus are called context menus or dropdown menus.

EXTERNAL PROGRAMS

You will need a few other programs to create a web site. They needn't be expensive or particularly advanced. A word editor, such as Word 2000 or even Windows Notepad, will do the trick. Although you can enter your text easily into Dreamweaver itself, you might wish to use your favourite word processor to do it. It's up to you, but if your text has been processed already you'll have less to do within your web building-programme.

A graphics manipulation program will help you modify your images to be fit for the Web. In this book, we have used another Macromedia product, Fireworks. It is a very intuitive program, fun to use and, as it is part of the Macromedia family, is fully compatible with Dreamweaver. If you do not wish to invest too much in external programs for your web pages, you could also get away with using the very reliable Windows Paint. If you want to use animated pictures (and you probably will at some point), it would be a good idea to search the Web for a free GIF animator. Try entering "Free GIF animator" in a search engine for a start.

© Copyright 1998–1999, Macromedia, Inc. All rights reserved.
Macromedia, the Macromedia logo, and Fireworks are trademarks or registered trademarks of Macromedia, Inc.
SalesAgent, Copyright 1996–1999 ReleaseNow.com, www.ReleaseNow.com. All Rights Reserved.

ICONIC TRICK

If you use Dreamweaver 3 a lot, you may want to bypass having to click on the Start button to launch it every time. Here is a windows trick: go to the folder where Dreamweaver 3 is stored (usually a folder called "Program Files\Macromedia\Dreamweaver 3" on your hard disk). Then right-click on Dreamweaver.exe and choose Create Shortcut. Now right-click on the shortcut created and choose Cut. Go somewhere on your desktop (your desktop is the area of the screen where no window is active), right-click again and this time choose Paste. You can either decide to click on this icon to launch Dreamweaver, or you can drag it onto your Taskbar to save space... This tip will work with any Windows 98 program.

START BUILDING

2

Once you have prepared your images and your text, it is time to start putting everything together. This is where you learn about titles, tables, colours, image formats, layers and much more besides. Creating your first web page can be as simple or as complicated as you want it to be. There are a few simple rules to follow and a few icons to get the hang of, but the rest is limited only by your imagination…

START A SITE

A site is the collection of folders in which your web files are stored, plus some extra information like where things will go in relation to each other and where everything will be placed on the Web. A site also acts as a reflection of the finished product that will eventually be available on the Web. Your site is half-created already – you have put all your images, sounds and other objects into folders.

You need to tell Dreamweaver 3 where your files are before you can start building a site. This is so that the program will automatically be able to link everything together easily when it comes to moving or adjusting your site. Do this by clicking on SITE/NEW SITE in the main menu bar. You will be presented with the Site Definition dialog box.

The Site Definition dialog box. Type in the path to your Local Root Folder (the folder in which all the images and various elements in your site are stored) or browse your hard disk for it by using the folder icon. Give your site a name that is easy to remember and relevant.

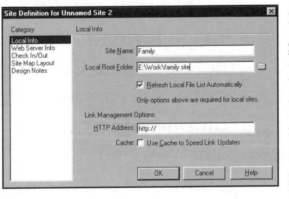

When you have filled all the details in, the Site Definition dialog box will contain all the information necessary for Dreamweaver 3 to manage your site. For now though, all you need to do is to name your site and select your root folder. Enter the information and click on OK to continue.

SITE DEFINING

If you have made a mistake, or if you want to modify any of your site location and definition details at this point, you can use the Define Site option accessed through the main menu bar (SITE/DEFINE SITE) to put everything right. From this box, select the site you need to modify (this will be the site you are working on) and select what you want to do with it. You can also create a New site, Edit a site, Duplicate or Remove existing ones. This window is available for you to use at any time while you are building your site. You will need to come back to this window when you start uploading your site on to a server (see Chapter 7).

Select the site you want to work on.

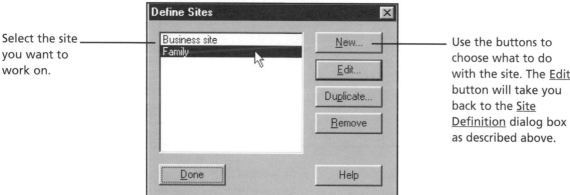

Use the buttons to choose what to do with the site. The Edit button will take you back to the Site Definition dialog box as described above.

The Define Sites dialog box is also used to select the site you are currently working on. If, say, you are working on both a professional and a private site, you can switch from one to the other without closing Dreamweaver 3 and opening it again. All the images and elements pertaining to one particular site will be available to you straight away and Dreamweaver 3 will remember where everything is for you.

IMPORTING SITES   _ 🗗 ✕

Dreamweaver can import sites that have been created by other programs. It will keep all of the site's information, which can be very useful, especially if you are upgrading from another web-building program. This feature is accessed using the FILE/IMPORT entry in the main menu bar.

SITE FILES

Once you have defined a site, you will be presented with the
Site window, specific to your site. This window will show you,
on the right-hand side, all the folders and all the files that make
up your site. On the left-hand side it shows all the files actually
currently available on the web).

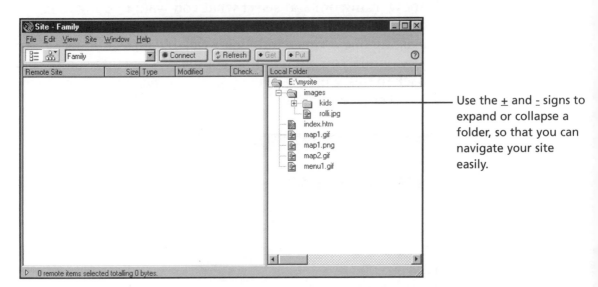

Use the + and - signs to
expand or collapse a
folder, so that you can
navigate your site
easily.

The Site dialog box is accessible throughout your web-
building session by either clicking on WINDOW/SITE FILES
in the main menu bar or by using the command key F5. You
will periodically need to come back to this dialog box to check
the "integrity" of your site (when putting together your
hyperlinks system, for example) but this window doesn't
really need to be visible all the time.

A NEW DOCUMENT

When you start Dreamweaver 3, you begin with an open,
blank document. If you need to open another one, either type
Ctrl+N or choose FILE/NEW from the main menu bar. To
open an existing document, choose FILE/OPEN (or Ctrl+O)
and to close a document select FILE/CLOSE (Ctrl+W). Note
that these are standard menus and shortcuts and are available
in most Windows 98 compatible programs.

ON THE GRID

To help you design your page, you can draw a grid that will cover it and give you useful markers: the placing of your images and text will be more accurate. This grid will not appear on your page when you view it with a web browser: it is just a guide for you to use to make sure that everything lines up.

Use the grid to help place elements accurately in your web pages.

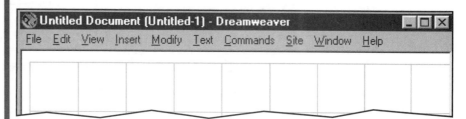

The grid is made up of horizontal and vertical lines appearing at an interval of 50 pixels. If you want a "tighter" grid, you can modify it by clicking on VIEW/GRID/SETTINGS... to get the Grid Settings dialog box. You can choose to have an invisible grid, but one that all your elements "snap" to (making alignment very easy), or you could have a visible grid with no "snap" if you just want to see your grid but not rely on it too much.

Toggle between a visible and an invisible grid while you work.

Choose a colour that will not blend with the background colour of your page so that you can see it clearly.

Activate the radio button to match the type of grid you need.

Change the interval between lines by entering a numerical value in this box.

For precise positioning of your elements, snap to the grid and select how close they are going to be from one another.

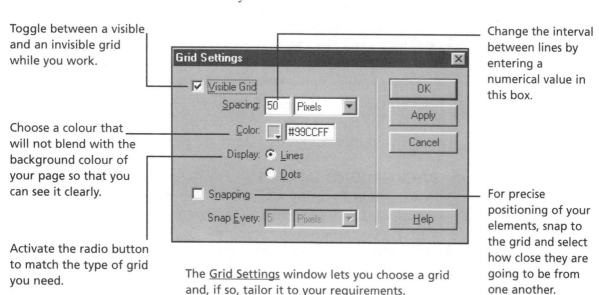

The Grid Settings window lets you choose a grid and, if so, tailor it to your requirements.

PAGE TITLES

Each page you create should have a title as well as an individual, recognizable file name. The page title is the writing that will be displayed in the title bar of your visitors' web browser.

If you do not give your page a name, it will be named, by default, Untitled-1.html. This is not very informative, and can be perceived as a lack of attention to detail on your part by the millions of people who are going to view your site on the web. Go to MODIFY/PAGE PROPERTY in the main menu bar or use Ctrl+J. This will bring up the Page Properties dialog box where you will be able to add a title to your page, as well as set up various other options.

BACKGROUND COLOURS

It is usually a good idea to add some colour to your web page. A coloured site can be very effective and nothing prevents you from matching your company's colours in your pages. If you choose a colour in the Page Properties dialog box, remember that all the graphics on this page will have to blend in with it: a pale blue background can be very nice, but will not be effective if most of your images are pale blue too.

BACKGROUND IMAGES

Instead of just adding a simple colour, you might wish to actually insert your company's logo (or your favourite picture) into it. You can do so by using the Background Image option in the Page Properties dialog box. One thing you will need to know, though: this image – when placed in the background –

will be tiled, which means it will be repeated horizontally and vertically in a pattern. This repetitive pattern can become a hindrance if the image is small because it will repeat so many times that it will become ineffective.

Because your image is going to be tiled, if you want your background to be a texture rather than a logo or picture, try to find (or to create) seamless images – usually known as textures. A seamless image will not show any unpleasant seams and lines on its borders when it is tiled.

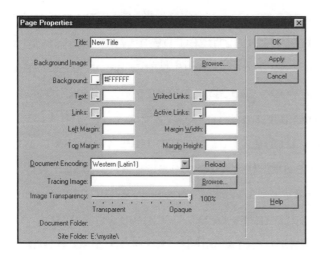

Use the options to select a background colour or a background image for your page. Once you have done that, save your page by selecting FILE/SAVE (Ctrl+S). By convention, the file name of the page your visitor will be taken to first when they visit your site should be "index.html".

The page property window. It is easy to adjust a lot of what is happening on each page from here. Enter the title of your page in the Title box. Try not to make it too long or obscure. "Welcome to the home page of Joe Bloggs' first, original and best web site" is obviously too long and will not be fully displayed in some people's browsers. Something like "Welcome" or "Joe Bloggs' Web Site" is concise and informative enough.

A single image of a canvas-type texture provides a nice, unobtrusive background.

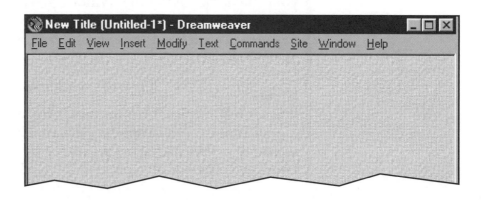

IMAGES ON THE WEB

You cannot just use any old image on your web site. Your images must be converted into specific file formats to be recognized by a web browser. The format of a graphic file is the way your image is coded by your graphic program. There are three acceptable formats for the web: GIF, JPEG and PNG. The other thing your image files will need to be is small. The smaller the file size, the faster your images will display in a web browser. Obviously you have a trade-off situation here, because you want your files to be as small as possible but you also want them to look as good as possible.

To recognize a file format, all you need to do is to look at the extension, or suffix (the three letters that appear at the end of your file name) of the file. Windows' basic graphic format is called a bitmap file and will be displayed as "image.bmp", for example. This format is not useful for the Web and will need to be changed.

JPEG
JPEG stands for Joint Photographic Experts Group. It is a highly-compressed image format capable of high quality for a reasonable file weight (the weight of an image is its size in kilobytes). The big plus point of JPEG files is that you can play

The file extension usually enables you to see which program created the file: here you can see that you have a Word document because the extension ".doc" is Microsoft Word's default file suffix.

This is the filename.

The ".gif" suffix tells you that this is a GIF file, and perfect for the Web.

This part, separated from the filename by a full point, is the file extension, or suffix.

The ".htm" extension shows that this is a Web page, readable by browsers and editable by web page creation software.

Name

- homepage.doc
- Celine.jpg
- macro10.JPG
- index.htm
- feedback.htm
- backgrd.gif
- blank.gif
- Martin.jpg

Here is the Adobe PhotoShop JPEG file saving option dialog box. As you can see, you can select how big your file is going to be and program gives you an idea of the quality of your image after it has been compressed.

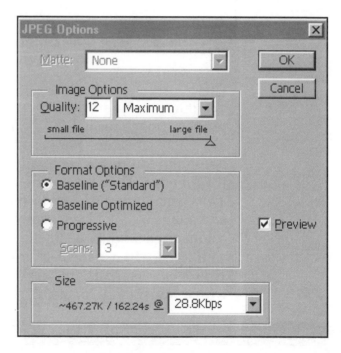

around with the level of compression to create bigger or smaller files (of better or worse quality) depending on your needs. But because, as is often the case, when you gain something, you lose something else, and the higher the level of compression, the more quality you lose.

As a general rule, you should use JPEG files when you need

an image to be of high quality, such as a photograph of a landscape or a portrait of a person. Experiment and save your picture using different compression levels to find a compromise between its weight and its quality. Most graphic programs (including Microsoft Paint) are capable of saving in JPEG format.

Above, to the left, is a transparent GIF file, with a white background. On the right is the same image, still transparent, on a textured background.

GIF

GIF (Graphic Interchange Format) is the all-round, multi-purpose image format for the Web. Because GIF files are extremely small, they are used for any kind of graphic that does not require the (generally photographic) quality of a JPEG image. They are mostly used to create buttons, lettering, icons, small graphics and also tiled backgrounds. A great advantage of GIF files is that you can assign a transparent colour to them (i.e. the image will not have a background colour – it will use the background colour of the web page). This is extremely useful, as you can create good visual effects with a transparent image, as shown above.

PIXELS

Digital images are made of a multitude of dots stuck together, called pixels. Each pixel corresponds to a colour. To get an idea of what a pixel looks like, look at a photograph through a magnifying glass: you will see that the photograph is made of thousands of coloured dots. A computer graphic works on exactly the same principle, although it is made up of a different base of colours from printed material (red, green and blue are the primary colours for televisions and monitors; red, blue and yellow are the primary colours for the print industry).

Transparency is particularly useful when your web page has an image for its background. Set the transparency of your GIF to the colour of your background and you will get a graphic that will blend perfectly with the rest of your page. Another feature of GIF files is that you can easily animate them.

All the graphic packages capable of saving as a GIF format will give you the option (when you are saving or exporting) of setting a colour for transparency of the image.

PNG

PNG (Portable Network Graphic) is a file format, which is a bit heavier than the GIF format. It is a relative newcomer to the Web and, unfortunately, is not compatible with all web browsers (only IE version 5 and Netscape version 5), which makes it a file format to use sparingly. Things move quickly, however, and it could soon be the new standard. A big advantage of PNG files is that you can make gradient transparencies with them and are not restricted to only one transparent colour as you are with a GIF.

PNG files are of very high quality and are recognized by most new versions of graphic packages.

OTHER FILE FORMATS

There is another file format that can be read by web browsers – TIFF (Tagged Information File Format) and you may see this on the Web sometimes. TIFF is the native graphic format for Macintosh computers, the same way Bitmap is for Windows. The Web develops very fast and new file formats appear all the time, but the three formats you learned about in these pages (plus, occasionally, TIFF) are sure to remain the standard ones for some time.

SEEING THE FILE FORMAT _ 🗗 ✕

If you can't see the extensions of your files, open your root directory within Windows and choose VIEW from the menu bar. Uncheck the box labelled "Hide file extensions" and click on OK. You will then be able to see all of the file types.

FILE SIZES

Why are there so many different file formats? Why do some make it and some do not? Why haven't Windows .BMP or PhotoShop .PSD become standards? The real answer to all of these can be summed up in one word: speed.

The main concern as far as web browsing is concerned is almost always speed. Because web browsing is done mostly through telephone lines, which are not always very fast by themselves, and because there are so many users at any point, your connection to the Web will fluctuate in speed. When you browse the Web, you are basically transferring files from one computer (the server) to another (your own computer) One way to speed things up (apart from having a very expensive internet connection) is to have smaller files to transfer. GIF, PNG, JPEG and TIFF are compressed file formats, which means that the image files are crunched and coded in a way that causes the files to become smaller. Other file formats are not compressed and therefore are much bigger – and unsuitable for the Web. In Web talk, fast is small and small is beautiful. Part of the beauty of the Web is that pictures only need to be displayed at a small resolution – 72dpi (dots per inch). Although this is fine for viewing images on a screen, it is no good for output or printing, which requires image sizes from about 300 to many thousand dpi. A 72dpi image

The same image, saved as a PNG and as a GIF. If you are waiting for an image to load, you'd rather wait for 16k.

map1.gif	16KB	GIF Image
map1.png	87KB	Macromedia Firewor...

contains just enough information to display an image perfectly on screen, but not to print it out clearly – as you may have noticed if you ever print web pages out. This doesn't matter, however, because you only want to be displaying your web pages on a screen. If you do want to put in higher-resolution files, you can make them easily downloadable via ftp.

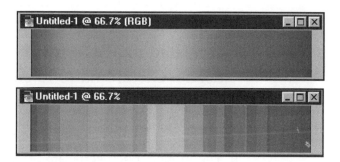

Two identical images saved in two different file formats: The image above is a PhotoShop PSD and the image below it is a GIF.

COLOURS

One way to reduce your file size is to put fewer colours in your images, or at least limit the number of colours that are used. Your web site will be viewed by a multitude of people on a multitude of machines, most of which will be slightly different. The colour palette that Windows PCs use is not the same as that of a Macintosh system, for example. The Web has its own set of 256 pre-defined, secure colours that will be seen correctly whatever platform you use. By reducing the number of colours to a maximum of those 256, you will create smaller files (because less information about colour will need to be stored in the file). GIF, PNG and TIFF are called indexed colour formats, because they can be restricted to use only Web secure colours.

One drawback to compression and colour restriction is, of course, loss of quality. If you want to display, say, a reproduction of a painting by Rembrandt in your page, choose JPEG instead of GIF because you will loose a lot less colour detail and overall quality. GIF is ideal for small graphics that do not contain a lot of colours.

ANIMATED IMAGES

You cannot use Dreamweaver 3 to build animated GIF images. Animated GIFs are the standard animated image format for use on the Web. You will need a GIF animator to create them. There are plenty to be found on the web for free.

Animated images are made with GIF images stuck together in a sequence. Each separate image (a frame) will be slightly different from the first, hence the animation. These images can be built using any graphic package that accepts GIF file format (they can even be built with 3D rendering programs if you are feeling really brave). You will only need a GIF animation program when all the separate frames have been created.

WHY USE ANIMATED GIFS?

Unfortunately, this book cannot show you animations. If it could, it might be slightly more entertaining, but that's why you want to build a web site. Animated GIFs are used to enhance a point, provide a bit of comic relief or a banner, amongst other things. They can be as garish or as subtle as you wish: it depends on the impact you want to create.

ANIMAGIC

Animagic is a shareware program that can be found at http://www.rtlsoft.com. It is quite complete and will create very effective animated GIFs.

In the main toolbar, you will find, under the EFFECT menu, a series of options to create quick animated GIFs by applying preset transitions to a couple of images.

There are heaps of GIF animators available on the Web – you do not have to use Animagic if you don't like the interface. Any of the others will do the job although some free software may not offer you the option to create transitions (interesting effects between frames). The thing to be careful about when creating animated GIFs is the weight of the final image: the file size of an animated GIF will amount to the sum of all the image files that make it. If you use big GIFs as a base for your animation, you will end up with an even bigger file. To remedy that, obviously try to work with small files to begin with and try to limit the number of colours they have. A black and white animation in a page full of colours can look very nice and be very quick to load.

1 Prepare your images, making each slightly different from the one before to create your animation.

Frame List
```
anim1.gif.000
anim2.gif.000
anim3.gif.000
anim4.gif.000
anim5.gif.000
```

2 In the <u>FILE</u> menu in the main menu bar, Select <u>Append Frames</u>. Choose the directory where the images needed for the animation are kept. They will be added to the <u>Frames List</u>.

3 A transition between two images. When you are happy with the animation that you have created, you will need to export or save your new animation, using the options from the <u>FILE</u> menu in the main menu bar.

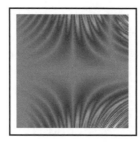

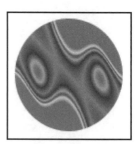

PHOTO ALBUMS

The <u>Photo Album</u> feature in Dreamweaver is very handy for creating – you guessed it – photo albums. Show Dreamweaver a folder with large, full-size images and it is capable of communicating with Fireworks to quickly create a photo album for you. This will, unfortunately, only work with Fireworks, and no other graphic manipulation programs.

1 Open the <u>Photo Album</u> dialog box by selecting <u>COMMANDS/CREATE WEB PHOTO ALBUM</u> from the main menu.

A photo album will be very useful to people who want to show a lot of images on the Web, for example a photographer showing work or a company showing products. If you loaded all of the images at once it would take ages to load and people would lose interest, so you display only small versions of your images (thumbnails) and when they are clicked on, the full image is displayed. This way people don't have to sit through hours of unnecessary downloads. To create a photo album, first you must select the images that you want processed. They will need to be full-size pictures, the type that are just that little bit too big to be viable to display on the web as they are (the idea is to give people the choice of viewing large pictures only if they want to). They can all be different sizes, though. Fireworks will use them and create a thumbnail version for you to put in your album.

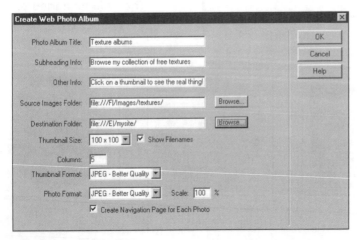

2 Clicking on a thumbnail of an imagel brings up the full photograph.

Click <u>OK</u> when all the information has been entered and watch Fireworks spring to life and batch process your image files. It may take a few minutes, depending on the number of images to process and on the speed of your computer.

Texture_miscrock_004.jpg   Texture_miscrock_005.jpg   Texture_miscrock_013.jpg

Dreamweaver will create a page with a table, the cells of which contain the thumbnails of your original, large images. Each of these thumbnails (if you chose the option <u>Create Navigation Page for Each Photo</u> in the <u>Create Web Photo Album</u> dialog box) will have a hyperlink to its own web page containing the full-size image. Not only that, but the new page will also contain its own navigation system!

3 Each new page has a navigation system that allows your visitor to view the previous and next image in the thumbnail table and well as going back to the original thumbnail page (the <u>Home</u> button).

Address 🔳 F \mysite\payes\~exture_miscrock_004_jpg htm

Texture albums/Texture miscrock 004.jpg

Back Home Next

If you decided not to create a navigation system when you set up your web photo album, you can still assign a hyperlink to each thumbnail. You can change anything you like in the pages that Dreamweaver has generated, for they have the same characteristics and properties of any other web page. The thumbnail table can be filled with colour, borders can be added, a new title and a background image can be inserted. One thing you can't do is change the filename of the thumbnail page: it must remain as index.html.

Placing Images

There was a time when web pages were linear: all you could do was place your images one after the other, without much control over their formatting, except for basic indentation (left, centre and right). Now you have a much better choice of where your images will appear on your pages. To be more creative and to ease exact placement of your pictures, it is best to use a layer.

Insert Image.

LAYERS

To create a layer, click on the <u>Draw Layer</u> icon in the <u>Objects</u> palette. Go back to your blank document and then click and drag a rectangle to the approximate size of your image. Then click on the <u>Insert Image</u> icon in the <u>Objects</u> palette and choose an image file. Your image will be inserted inside your layer. Clicking the <u>Insert Image</u> button takes you to the <u>Select Image Source</u> dialog box, from which you can pick the image you need. If you make a mistake, simply double-click on the image to go back to the <u>Select Image Source</u> dialog box and change it. To delete an image, click on it and press <u>Delete</u> on your keyboard.

Insert Layer.

Layers can contain any file that will be recognized by web browsers, be they images, animated GIFs, tables or text. A layer can be moved around your page and the image inside it will follow.

Click on the square on the top left to move your layer to its desired position. This is also where you should click to select a layer. You can use the sizing handles (the black boxes) to resize your layer.

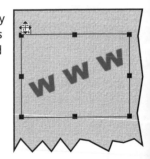

MORE INFORMATION

Once an image is selected (by clicking on it), the <u>Property Inspector</u> will come into action, providing you with useful information.

The file size of your image (its weight).

If you want to change the source file for your image (change the image), click on the folder icon to select a new image.

Enter a name for your image for quick reference.

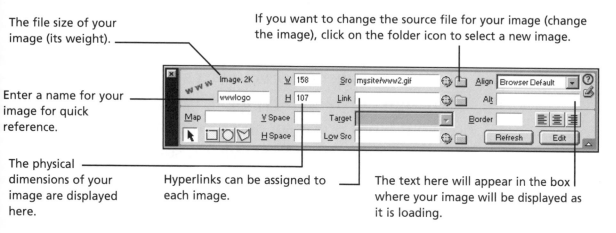

The physical dimensions of your image are displayed here.

Hyperlinks can be assigned to each image.

The text here will appear in the box where your image will be displayed as it is loading.

If you click on the layer, the <u>Property Inspector</u> will change to display the layer properties rather than those of the image. As for the image, give it a proper name and check its dimensions.

Give your layer a name.

If the design of your page requires it, you can fill your layer with a background colour or a background image. Click on the <u>Bg Color</u> box or browse your root directory for a background picture. When working with layers, you must be careful not to overlap them: some, particularly older, browsers do not accept this kind of arrangement. If you find it difficult to place your layers accurately so that they don't overlap, ask Dreamweaver to do it for you: have <u>VIEW/PREVENT LAYER OVERLAPS</u> ticked in the main menu bar. Another option you may want to take advantage of is <u>Snap to Grid</u> from <u>VIEW/GRID/SNAP TO</u>. This will easily align your layers to the grid.

WORKING WITH TEXT

You can either enter your text straight into your web design program by typing it, or you can write it in your word processor and then paste it into your page, only with this drawback: some formatting or layout options from your word processor will not be recognized.

To insert it into your page, you do with your text what you did with your images: put it in a layer so that you can place it exactly where you want. Once you have created a layer for your text, simply click inside it and start typing or paste your prepared text into it. If you resize your layer, the text will wrap automatically to match its new dimensions.

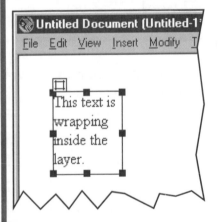 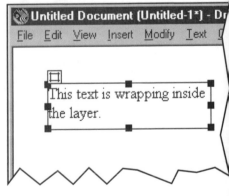

An example of a text layer wrapping automatically. You can drag the layer and adjust its size using the handles.

Click on these buttons to align the text inside a
layer to the left, to the right or to centre it.

Your text can be
bold or italic.

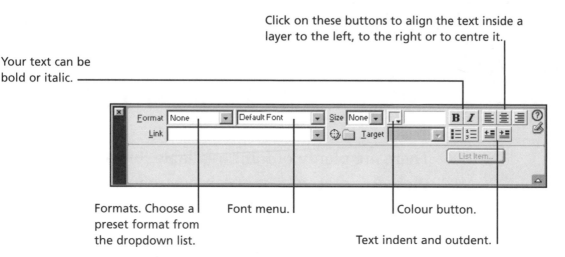

Formats. Choose a
preset format from
the dropdown list.

Font menu.

Colour button.

Text indent and outdent.

To indent a whole paragraph to the left, click on the Text Indent button until
you are satisfied with its position. The Text Outdent button will move the
selected paragraph the other way.

Refer, once again, to the Properties Inspector to change the way
your text is displayed (as for all Windows-compatible
programs, the icons and options available from a toolbar can be
accessed through a menu item: in the case of text, it is the TEXT
entry in the main menu bar).

You can have bulleted or numbered lists. Select the type of list
you want by clicking on the button and enter your text. A new
entry will be created every time you hit the Enter key and start
a new paragraph.

Each individual letter in your text can be of a different colour
(if you really want). Select the text you want to change the
colour of and click on the colour palette button. Change the
font of your text from the (limited) selection.

MANY HARD RETURNS

When you hit the Enter key, you will see that there is quite a gap between the end of your previous
paragraph and the beginning of the new one. This is because you have just inserted a hard return and
they are automatically assigned a full line break. To bypass this empty horizontal line, type Shift+Enter
instead of a straight Enter. This will produce a soft return that will make your new paragraph start
exactly one line below the previous one, with no break.

WORKING WITH FONTS

There are plenty of fonts available for free on the Web. Alternatively, you can buy whole collections of fonts on CD. You might find that one of these fonts will be the one that will be absolutely perfect for your page. So you use it and it looks very nice on your page. There is one problem though – the chances are that nobody but you will be able to see the text in that particular font.

The folder WINDOWS/FONTS/ on your main hard disk will contain all the fonts available on your system. Double-click on one to see what it looks like.

The problem is that fonts are not embedded in web pages. This means that any text you enter will be displayed on your visitor's web browser using only the fonts that are installed on their computer, in their browser. If your visitor does not have the font you used, another one will be substituted automatically and a lot of things could go wrong. Your text could be too big, too small or not blend properly with your images – it could even overlap them.

Fonts are collections of characters (the alphabet, numbers, numeric and other symbols) that have the same style. Fonts are divided into "families" (groups), but the basic differentiation is between serif fonts and sans serif fonts. Serif fonts have small horizontal bars at the end of the main bars that build them. Sans serif do not.

A sans serif font (Arial) and a serif font (Times New Roman).

Traditionally, serif fonts are used for the body text in books and newspapers. Sans serif fonts are often used for headlines but are often seen as less formal. Sans serif fonts are easier to transform into graphics – see the box below – because they don't have extra horizontal bars.

TEXT OR TEXT GRAPHIC?

If there is a really exotic font you want to use in your site but you are sure nobody will have it installed on their computer, do not despair – cheat. Instead of typing your text using the font in your web design program, type it in your favourite graphic package and save the text as a transparent image. With a bit of experimentation, you will manage to blend the image of your text in your page so that it doesn't look like an image at all, but like "proper" text. Of course you can use this technique with any font, even a Web default one if you really want to. Bear in mind, though, that a "text picture" takes up as much room as a picture, which is a lot more room than just plain text.

FONT SIZES

When you have selected some text you will notice a <u>Size</u> button in the <u>Properties Inspector</u>. If you click on it, you will get a list of font sizes. These are not point sizes, as you would find in a word processor, but standard web font sizes. These are quite limited in their sizing capabilities but they do ensure that everyone will look at the same size font when they access your pages.

The options for changing the font size are quite different from those in a word processor.

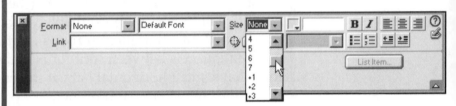

The default font size in Dreamweaver is 3 . It will appear as "none" in the <u>Size</u> box of the <u>Properties</u> palette. It is roughly equal to 12-point size in a word processor. In HTML font sizes are said to be relative, which means simply that two is smaller than three, four is bigger than three, and so on. This is because of the massive variety of machines that will be used to viewing web pages. As seen in the illustration above, you change the font size in steps of one. The sizes are also cumulative in that you can add two to a font size of three to make a font size of five. The same principle applies to decreasing the font size. If you know the font size you want to use, simply select it from the dropdown menu or input the value in the <u>Size</u> box.

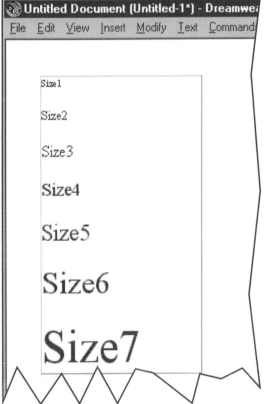

The seven font sizes available when you work with text in any given web design program.

TYPES OF FONTS

Dreamweaver 3 use two types of font, depending on what it has to display. Proportional fonts are used for text in paragraphs, headings, and tables. The default for this is Times New Roman 12 point on Windows and Times 12 point on the Macintosh. Fixed fonts – used in all other situations such as form elements – are displayed in Courier New 10 point on Windows machines and Courier 12 point on Macs. This does not necessarily mean that these will be the fonts or the font sizes your visitors will automatically see on their screen when they browse your site, however. They will only be displayed in this way primarily if the visitor has the fonts installed on their machine. Also, there are ways for every user to modify the font they use while browsing the Internet and you, as a web site builder, have no control over the settings of your visitor's web browser preferences. Nevertheless, as you cannot create a site for all the font sizes your visitors might choose to use as defaults, you should simply work with the default sizes, and for those who get a strange display there will be millions of others who will get a perfect site.

As you can see in the illustration, working with text is not as easy at it could (and certainly should) be in web design. You have to be wary of the fact that different systems will display your site in a different way. The form element you have painstakingly positioned in your page to match the position of an image using the Windows version of Dreamweaver 3 will not display as you meant it to when viewed on a Macintosh machine. The way to avoid that is to create a JAVA switch to automatically view which browser your visitors are using and to redirect them to a proper Windows or Macintosh version of your site.

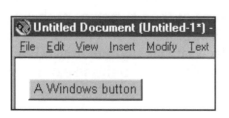

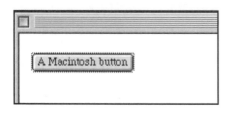

The font used to display different elements in your page will not always appear the same. The same font on a Windows system (top) and on a Macintosh system (above).

USING TABLES

Tables in web site-building are just like tables in spreadsheet, database and word processing programs. They are a collection of "cells" arranged in a specific way with elements inside them such as text or images.

The only difference is that you cannot make any calculations in a table in a web design program the way you can with, say, Microsoft Excel. Tables are used to hold elements and lock them into place. They work a different way from layers, though, and can solve some of the placement problems that layers have (such as the impossibility of centring a layer on a page). Once a layer is placed it stays where it is, while a table can adjust itself on screen according to the size of the web browser's window.

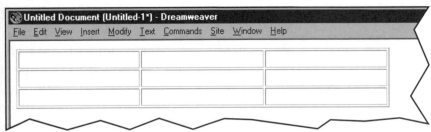

Each web element will be placed into a separate cell of this empty table.

1 Go to the Objects toolbar and click once on the Insert Table button.

To insert a table into your HTML document, first click where you want the table to go inside your document and then select the Insert Table button in the Objects palette. For now, do not place your table in a layer, but simply inside your main document.

As soon as the <u>Insert Table</u> button is pressed, you will get the <u>Insert Table</u> dialog box, from where you can specify the appearance of your table.

2 Select the relative size of your table, and the number of rows and columns in it. Enter the total width of your table. A 100 <u>Percent</u> value will span the entire width of your document if you want to specify a percentage rather than a fixed pixel width.

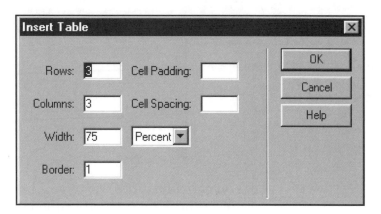

Use the various fields to build your table to your specifications and click <u>OK</u>. You will be be able to modify these values later on. Now that your table has been placed, the <u>Properties Inspector</u> has become the <u>Table Properties Inspector</u>.

3 The <u>Table Properties Inspector</u>, used to modify your table and its elements.

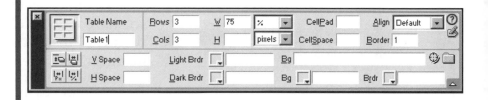

SPLITTING AND MERGING

An important option is the ability to merge or split the cells in your table. Use the <u>Split</u> and <u>Merge</u> buttons to create the perfect table according to the elements that are going to go into it. Splitting a cell means that a particular cell will be divided into a number of smaller sub-cells. First click inside the cell you wish to split and then click on the <u>Split Cell</u> button in the <u>Table Properties Inspector</u>. This will bring up the <u>Split Cell</u> dialog box.

The <u>Split Cell</u> icon is highlighted. The <u>Merge Cell</u> icon is next to it.

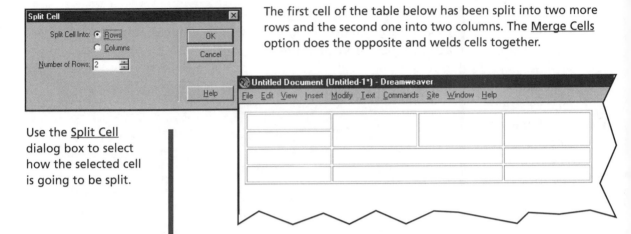

The first cell of the table below has been split into two more rows and the second one into two columns. The Merge Cells option does the opposite and welds cells together.

Use the Split Cell dialog box to select how the selected cell is going to be split.

You can adjust the width and height of your table by placing your mouse on the end or the bottom of it. The pointer will change into a double vertical or horizontal bar. When the mouse pointer is like this, click and drag your table border to its new dimensions. You can also enter numerical values in the Table Properties Inspector (in the W and H boxes and their dropdown list, which you have already seen on page 46 in the Insert Table dialog box).

Splitting and merging cells is a way to add or remove the smaller cells in your table. You may also need to add or delete an entire row or column. To do so, first right-click inside a cell. A dropdown menu (context menu) will appear. Choose the action you want to perform on your table from the list.

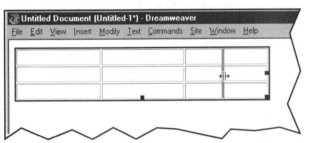

Fine-tune your table's dimensions manually by dragging on the lines inside it. This applies to individual columns and rows as well.

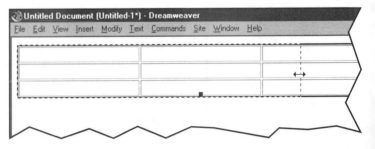

COLOUR YOUR CELLS

Each cell in a table can be assigned its own colour. This is useful to draw attention to important elements. You can also put a frame around cells. For the former, click inside the cell you wish to colour and click on the <u>Colour</u> button in the <u>Table Properties Inspector</u>. This brings up the colour palette.

Select a colour for the particular cell. Repeat these steps for each cell you want to colour.

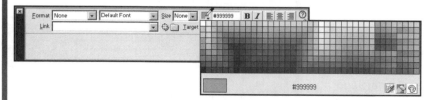

The table, by default, comes with a border, the width of which is specified in the border field in the <u>Table Properties Inspector</u>. If you do not want a border around your table, set the border value to 0. You can create a 3D effect with the border by assigning a set of two colours to it, the <u>Light</u> and <u>Dark Brdr</u> colours. Right-click inside any cell and choose <u>Select Table</u> in the menu that appears. The <u>Light</u> and <u>Dark Brdr</u> colours buttons will appear in the <u>Table Properties Inspector</u>. Select a different colour for each and hit <u>Enter</u>.

Use the colour palettes for a 3D effect.

FILLING TABLES

Once your table is built, you will need to fill it with images or text. To do this you can either click inside the relevant cell and start typing, or click the <u>Insert Image</u> button on the <u>Objects</u> palette as if you were inserting an image into a layer.

CELL COLOUR BUG

If you do assign a colour to a single cell, make sure that the cell is not completely empty (there should either be some text or an image in it). Because of a bug in some web browsers, the colour may not actually be visible. If nothing is supposed to be in this cell, place a tiny transparent image in it to remedy the problem.

Each of the elements placed inside a cell can be aligned and indented in the same way they can be in a layer. Simply select the cell and go to the <u>Horizontal</u> and <u>Vertical</u> fields in the <u>Table Properties Inspector</u> to set the alignment you need from the dropdown menus. The whole table can also be aligned by selecting it and changing the alignment in the <u>Align</u> field in the <u>Table Properties Inspector.</u>

Set the way your images and text will be aligned within cells by using the <u>Horz</u> and <u>Vert</u> fields.

Set the alignment for the whole table when you have selected it.

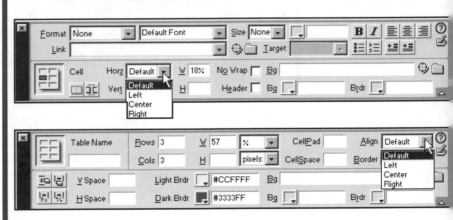

SEPARATORS

You will notice that your table will automatically centre itself (or align itself to the left or right, depending on your alignment settings), when you make your document window bigger or smaller. This is the way the table will appear in your visitor's web browser. Empty cells can appear very small when the table wraps like this. To remedy this problem, it is often useful to place a separator in an empty cell between two filled cells. A separator is just a small transparent image, the width of which will be the width of the gap you need between two cells. The alternative to this technique is to use <u>CellPad</u> and CellSpace.

Use the <u>CellPad</u> and <u>CellSpace</u> options to fine-tune the cells in your table. For the former, specify a value in pixels for the gap between the content of the cell and its borders (walls). For <u>CellSpace</u>, the value specifies the distance in pixels from one cell from another.

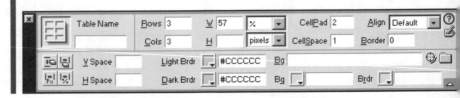

INTERACTIVE SITES

3

A site is much more than just a collection of web pages. Once your pages have been created, you will need to link them together to build a complete site. To do so, you have powerful tools – hyperlinks – at your disposal. Not only can you link pages together so that your visitor can easily navigate the whole of your site; you can use them to trigger a request for an email or the download of a file.

WHAT ARE HYPERLINKS?

A hyperlink (or just plain link) is an instruction that will cause your browser to jump to another file, usually another web page, the way you would flick to a given page when you read a book. A system of links is the "nervous system" of a site. They can be made either with text or images and can point to a wide variety of your, or other, documents. When you view a web site, a link is easily recognizable when the mouse changes from an arrow to a pointed finger. One piece of advice for when you are building your site: it is far easier to have the page you want to link to ready before you create the link.

This is the error page you never want to see. It appears whenever you have linked to a file that is not available.

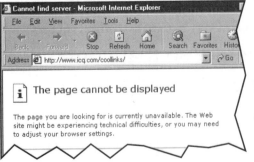

TYPES OF HYPERLINK

Links come in two types: internal and external. Internal links point to pages that are part of your own web site. External links point to pages that are hosted on another site. The important thing about the latter is that you must make sure that their address is accurate and that it will not change. If it does and your visitor clicks on the outdated link on your page, an error message will appear saying that the page they wanted to view is no longer available – very unprofessional. If you do use external links, check their relevance from time to time and update your pages accordingly.

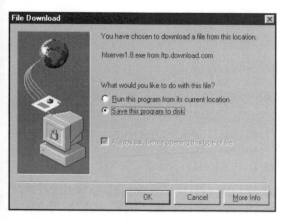

If a link points to a file format that your web browser doesn't recognize, you will get this window asking you what to do with it. It is often safer, when you download such a file, to save it to disk and then run a virus check on it.

LINKABLE FILES

A link doesn't have to just point to another web page. You can have a link that goes to a downloadable file. It can link to any type of file: image, program, sound file and so on. If the file you point to has been set up with a "helper" in your visitor's browser (helpers are programs associated with certain types of files), then it will be processed and displayed correctly. If it is an archive file (or a file that is not associated with a helper), the viewer will get a window asking for instructions: do they want to save this file to disk or choose an application to run it? It is easy for the user to choose what to do, and how to do it from here.

A link is a request from your page to transfer a document from a remote computer (i.e. another web site) to yours. This transfer operation is called a download. Internet Explorer5 (IE5) comes with a download manager, which runs in the background, to help you keep track of the files you transfer. Other Web browsers and previous versions of IE will present you with a small window detailing the download process.

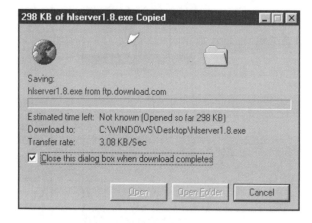

Each time you link to a file that is not an HTML file, you will get a Download Status window.

LINKING TEXT

The most basic link is a text link. To create a link from a piece of your text to something or somewhere else, first use the mouse to highlight the words you want to create a link from.

When this is done, use the Link box in Dreamweaver's Properties palette. Use the folder icon next to the Link box to browse for the file you wish to link to or, if you know the address, just fill it in.

Another method to establish links between pages or other files is to use Dreamweaver's Point to File feature. First, open your Site Files window (F5). Expand or collapse the folders using the plus and minus signs until you find the file you want to point to. Then click on the Point to File icon and drag the dotted line to the file you need. Your link is automatically created.

If you use external links, be sure to type the complete URL (Uniform Resource Locator – the address) in the URL field. It should look something like: "http://www.domain name/page name.htm" (or .html). If you use an internal link, your web design package will sort

Click on the folder icon to select a file to link to, or if you are sure you know it exactly, type in the address of the link.

The Point to File icon.

out where it is in relation to the calling page by itself. Paths (the locations of your files) are very important at this stage. Make sure the layout of your sitewill not change. If you move a file, the link to this file will be rendered obsolete and your visitor will get an error message (the dreaded "File not Found") because their web browser will attempt to transfer a file to you from a "false" address.

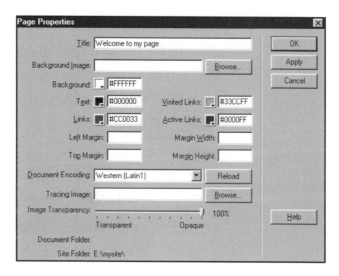

LINK COLOURS

Once the link has been activated, the selected text will change colour and will be underlined. You can change the colour of the text link by opening the Page Properties dialog box, accessed through MODIFY/PAGE PROPERTIES... in the main menu bar or by using the keyboard shortcut Ctrl+J.

Text: the colour for normal (unhighlighted) text throughout your page.

Links: the colour of text that links elsewhere throughout your page.

Visited Links: the colour that linked text will become when you have visited the link (to help your visitor navigate).

Active Links: shows that you have clicked on a link and that you are still on the page it points to.

To change a colour, click on the square next to each item to modify it. The box will display the colour's code.

LINKING IMAGES

You can create hyperlinks from images the same way you can create hyperlinks with text. The image of a button that says "Sales" or "Contact", for example, will be more effective than just a line of text pointing to the same address. Also, you can divide an image into smaller portions and have what is called an image map to create more than one hyperlink from a single image. This is ideal when you have a large picture that explains everything there is to see in the site, because you can leave some elements of this picture "blank" (with no link) whereas others can be "live".

The procedure to follow for creating a link from a graphic is the same as for a text link: it is a case of selecting the image by clicking on it and entering the relevant information in the Properties Inspector. Click on the small down arrow on the right-hand side of this box to expand it and have access to more options.

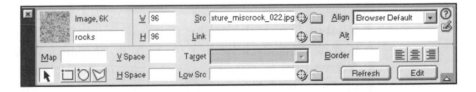

If you want to use a border (to specify that this image is a link, for instance), this is where you set its width by specifying a value. You must set the border value to 0 if you do not want a border.

IMAGE MAPS

Another way to create a link is to use an image map. This is particularly useful when you have an image that can be divided into smaller images, like this one:

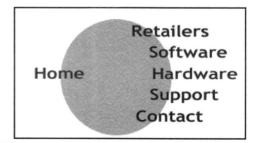

This could be the logo of a company dealing with computers, for instance. Using an image map would be perfect to aid navigation with this image. Click on it and check out the shape tools in the <u>Image Properties Inspector</u>.

1 Select a shape tool and give your map a name in the box.

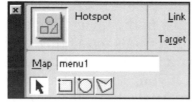

2 Draw a shape around the portion of the image you want to use as a hyperlink.

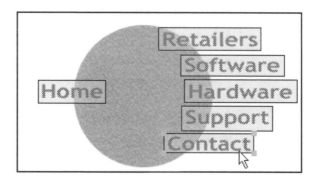

Now go back to your image and add "hotspots" to it. The hotspots are the areas on the image that will become links. In this example, each menu item is associated with (and will eventually link to) a different web page.

ADDRESSES

The same conventions regarding addresses for external links can be followed when you create links from text, images or image maps.

3 You can move the hotspot, or you can resize it using the sizing handles.

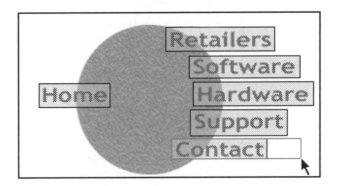

You can move and resize your hotspots by clicking on the black arrow in the <u>Image Properties Inspector</u> and then on the hotspot that needs modifying. Hold down the mouse button and drag it to a new position or use the sizing handles to resize it. If you are not satisfied with a hotspot, simply click on it and hit <u>Delete</u>. If, on the other hand, you fall in love with it, you can copy and paste it to a new location as many times as required.

Once a hotspot has been defined, the <u>Property Inspector</u> will change to reflect the fact that you have it selected. You will need to fill in links and other information.

You are not restricted to regular, four-sided shapes for your hotspot. In this example, you could have done without the "Home" button and used the whole circle as a hotspot.

4 Create different-sized hotspots using the different shape tools.

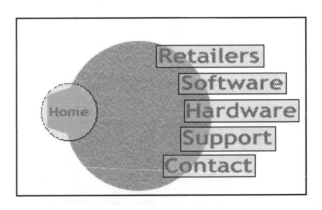

The <u>Hotspot</u>
<u>Properties</u>
<u>Inspector</u>.

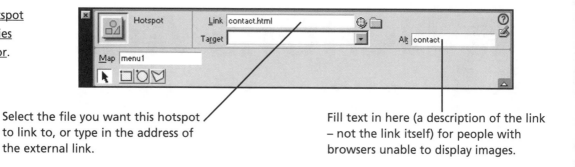

Select the file you want this hotspot
to link to, or type in the address of
the external link.

Fill text in here (a description of the link
– not the link itself) for people with
browsers unable to display images.

PRECAUTIONS

It is not a good idea to create too many hotspots in a single
image, unless they are well spaced out. It is not advisable to
overlap hotspots either, as this will create confusing links and
may even cause web browsers to crash. Use image maps for
large images and images that can be clearly and easily divided
into smaller portions. Although you won't be allowed to draw
shapes outside the image, you can draw shapes slightly larger
than the items they define. This way you make it easy for your
visitors: if you draw very small shapes, they may be difficult
to select.

This image contains complex text work, but an image map can still be assigned
to it. Use the line tool instead of the conventional rectangle one and draw
your shapes carefully.

OTHER PROGRAMS

All major web design programs will offer you the possibility of creating image maps. The icons and
dialog boxes will be different, but the process and the conventions (naming your map, typing complete
URLs etc.) will remain the same no matter which program you are using.

ANCHORS AND NEW WINDOWS

If you create a very long web page, you might want to give your visitor the possibility of navigating the page itself – otherwise they will have to scroll the page down and then up again, running the risk of losing themselves or getting confused along the way. Remember: a site must be as user-friendly as possible. It is this kind of attention to detail that will make a site easy and pleasurable to navigate.

1 Bring up the Invisibles option in the Objects palette by selecting the down arrow on the right.

Links from one position in a page to another position in the same page are made using anchors. Anchors, in Dreamweaver 3, are found in the Objects palette. At the top of the palette, you will see "Common" written in the Objects tab. Click on the tab to get a dropdown menu and select Invisibles from the list. The anchor icon, amongst other things, will be available from this tab. We'll only deal with the anchor option for now.

To link to an anchor from some text or a picture, you first define a position on your page as an anchor and then you link to that anchor as you would any other link. To do this, position your cursor where you want the anchor to be and click on the Anchor icon in the Invisibles palette. This brings up the Insert Named Anchor dialog box into which you should type the name for your anchor. The name should not contain any spaces. Use lowercase lettering and lines instead of spaces: "first_anchor" for example. Try to find short, relevant names for each and every one of your anchors, of a maximum of 26 letters.

As soon as you click the anchor icon, the <u>Insert Named Anchor</u> dialog box appears. If you click on an anchor once it has been set, the <u>Properties Inspector</u> will turn into the <u>Anchor Properties Inspector</u> from which you will be able to modify the name of your anchor if you need to. To link to an anchor, click the element that you want to link from (some text or an image) and type the special character "#" (the hash key) followed by the name of the anchor.

2 Type the name of your anchor in the <u>Insert Named Anchor</u> dialog box.

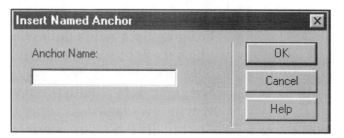

To link to an anchor, type in the character # followed by the name of the anchor you want to point to.

The anchor will be attached to a piece of text or an image, usually in a layer, and will move with it. The element associated with an anchor (the part of the page you have linked to), when clicked on by a web browser, will appear right at the top of the page. The symbol of the anchor, as seen by you when you are creating the page, will not appear at all. A very common use for an anchor is to link back to the top of a page, or to specific points in a page such as subheadings. It can be very effective to build a small image, or have some text that says "Top" so that your visitor can go back to the top of the page from anywhere else in your page (provided you have an anchor there, of course).

ANCHORS IN OTHER PAGES

Anchors work with text, images and image maps. You can also make a link that points to an anchor on another page: simply add # and the name of the anchor in that page after the page name in the <u>Link</u> box (i.e: index.html#anchorname) in the <u>Image Properties</u> or <u>Text Properties Inspector</u>.

BRINGING UP NEW WINDOWS

Sometimes, it is easier and more convenient to bring up a whole new window with a link rather than just calling up a new page in the same browser window. This is particularly useful when you want to link an element to another web site that someone else has built: the new window will open the new site but your own site will still be available to your viewer. It is also a bonus if you want to show off a particular page in your site – a full-size image, for example – and still provide your visitor with your main menu navigation options.

Bringing up a new window is done through a palette that we haven't yet used, the Behaviors palette. If this palette is not visible, open it via WINDOW/BEHAVIORS or by pressing F8.

The Behaviors palette gives you control over the creation of new windows (amongst other things). Strictly speaking, these are not really links you are going to work with now, but Actions. They are JAVAScript codes that will be embedded into your HTML code – but don't worry, you won't have to learn, or even deal with, any programming.

THE BEHAVIORS PALETTE

Because we are not dealing with HTML any more, you will have to select which browser the actions will be available for. A problem that the Internet has been faced with through its whole existence is that of compatibility. Getting everybody to make their browsers capable of reading the same things in the same way will always be difficult. Unfortunately this means that you are faced with a choice: do you build a page that you know will be easily read by pretty much anybody on any machine, or do you build a page that will be read by fewer people? Sounds like an easy choice, but the page that fewer people can read will look nicer, probably contain all sorts of interesting things like sound and animation and will be much more interactive. You need to decide whether your target audience will be using the latest browsers or not (many people will be – they are free, after all!) and add behaviours to your pages accordingly. At this stage, your best idea is probably to leave the Dreamweaver default value: "4 and Later browsers".

Once you have clicked on the element of your web page that you want to trigger the action (the Event), click on the + button to bring down the list of events you can associate this element with (you can click the - sign to delete an action you are not satisfied with later on).

Your window can have as many or as few details as you wish. If it contains a picture that you want to be displayed full-size in the window (for instance) and that you don't want people to adjust, don't allow any resizing handles on your new window. Opening new windows is a technique used a lot with thumbnails. Link a thumbnail (a small version of an image) to its full-size match in a popup window for good effects.

1 When you have selected the element of your page that you want to trigger the action, open the <u>Behaviors</u> palette and select the web browser(s) that you want your action to be compatible with.

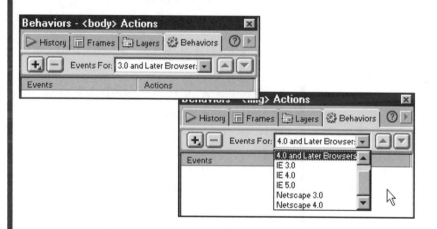

2 Select the <u>Open Browser Window</u> action. When your visitor performs the required Event, a new window will open (this is the Action).

3 Enter the specifications for your new window in the <u>Open Browser Window</u> dialog box that appears. You can specify the size of your new window in pixels and you can tailor your new window and give it only the function tools you want it to have.

G ETTING IN TOUCH

One great aspect of a web site is that it can bring you near-instantaneous feedback from your visitors. By just clicking on a line of text or an image, they can be given the option of sending you information, comment or encouragement. This is, in many ways, what the Internet is all about.

The easiest way to get feedback is with what is known as a mailto. It is a small piece of code that uses your visitor's browser to send you an email. Setting up a mailto is extremely simple. If you can build a hyperlink (and if you've read this far, you can!), you can build a mailto: it is just a matter of knowing the email address of the person you wish to contact.

You can set multiple mailtos in a single page: this is ideal to contact the relevant department of a company or even a particular person in a department.

Sales, Service and General can each assigned their ow mailto in this ima but they will nee be hotspots.

To create a mailto, first select the image, hotspot or piece of text that will serve as a base for the link. In the relevant <u>Properties</u> inspector, instead of typing a hyperlink, type the email address of the person you want the email to be sent to, preceeded by "mailto:". A mailto works like an ordinary link, but instead of triggering the display of a new web page, it runs your visitor's e-mail program.

Anything that can be used in a web page to create a hyperlink can be used to create a mailto.

The mailto will open a new message by activating your visitor's email editor. Once the message has been written and sent (the visitor gets to decide whether to send you the email or not), depending on your visitor's preferences and setup, the message will be sent.

A message window from Outlook 2000, part of the Office 2000 package. Most people who send email send it with Outlook.

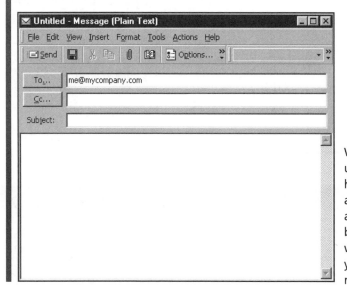

With a mailto, the user's name will have been automatically added to the email by their browser, as will the address you specify in the mailto.

Check your site links with the Check Links Sitewide window.

A LAST LOOK AT LINKS

Extra care should be taken when building hyperlinks. If the structure of your site is clear, your links will be very easy to set up. If not, you may run into problems so check your links one by one. Dreamweaver 3 is ready to help you by performing a check of your links for you. Hit Ctrl+F8 to bring up the Check Links Sitewide window (or choose SITE/CHECK LINKS SITEWIDE from the main menu bar). This feature will read all the HTML files in your site and check whether any links are broken (the web designer's term for "not working"). If they are, the offending files and the missing links within them will be listed.

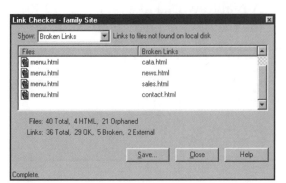

Another way to check the integrity of your site is to use the Site Map feature, called up by Ctrl+F5. Each HTML file will be displayed in the style used by Windows 98 Explorer and you can use the + and - signs to expand and collapse the links. Linked files will be joined by a black line. In a window to the right of this, your site's position on your computer is shown.

The Site Map will show you the structure of your links system.

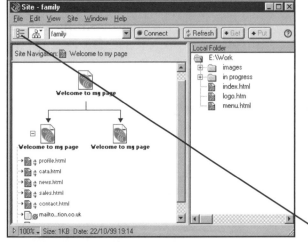

Click here to go to the Site Files window. You can upload your site from here.

VIEWING LINKS ONLINE

When you pass your mouse over a link, be it a text link, an image link, an image map or a mailto, you will notice, at the bottom of your web browser, the full URL of the file – or email address – that this link points to. This can be useful when checking your site or wondering why a link STILL doesn't work.

BIGGER SITES

4

Now that you have created a basic site, the time has come to take a further step and add a little functionality and some effects to your pages. These new functions include frames, rollovers, animations and sound effects. A combination of these can make your site look much more professional and easier to navigate. Don't forget, though, that your aim is still a clear, easy-to-access and entertaining site.

USING FRAMES

A frame is a web page inside a web page. Frames are usually used to create easily navigable tables of contents and menus. In a classic frame site you get a menu in one part of your screen and the pages the menu relates to in the other.

The advantage of a framed site as described above is that the menu in a frame can always be present. It only needs to be loaded once, and it stays on screen when the selected menu options are accessed, so although the content of your site changes, the navigation system doesn't. This makes the navigation of your site faster and easier. All major web-building programs allow you to create framesets, the common name for a set of frames.

FRAMESETS

The home page of a site is usually called index.html. In most framesets the home page is actually made up of three other, separate pages: the page index.html itself, the menu page called menu.html (in the left frame) and the introduction page called intro.html (in the right frame). All the hyperlinks in menu.html point to pages that will be displayed in the frame on the right, so when the person looking at your site clicks on one of the links in menu.html the only part of the page that will change is the right-hand side. The page intro.html will be replaced by another page. The page index.html forms a frameset.

SETTING UP A FRAMESET

To create a frame you will need to go to the <u>Objects</u> palette and click on the top right button to access the dropdown list. Select <u>Frames</u> from this list.

1 Select <u>Frames</u> from the list to change the <u>Objects</u> palette to a frame inserter. Then click on the frames you want to insert in your page.

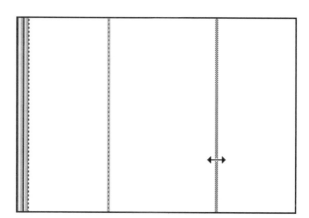

2 If you need to resize a frame, place your mouse over one of the lines and wait for it to change into a set of opposing arrows. When it does so, you can drag the frame left, right, up or down (depending on whether it is a horizontal or vertical one).

3 Add a border to your frame, set its width and colour. Enter numerical values for the width of the frame, in percent or pixels. Click in the box on the right to select a frame.

In your web page, the frames that you have chosen to insert will be displayed as dotted lines. If you need to delete a frame, simply drag the dotted line to one of the borders of your display window until it disappears. Dreamweaver will ask you whether you want to save the frameset before you do this, in case you are making a mistake. Each time you select a frame, the <u>Properties Inspector</u> changes into the <u>Frame Properties Inspector</u>. Use the inspector to adjust the various settings for your frameset such as borders, border colours and the sizes of the frames.

NAME THAT FRAME

One important thing with frames is that they need to be named. Use a name that doesn't contain any spaces and use no more than 26 characters. To name your frames, go to the <u>Frames Properties Inspector</u>. When you are working with frames and want to easily navigate between different ones, bring up the <u>Frames</u> tab with <u>Ctrl+F10</u> or choose <u>WINDOW/FRAMES</u> in the main menu bar. You will see a small version of the frameset on the left of the window.

The <u>Frames Properties Inspector</u>. From here you can name your frames and change many of their attributes.

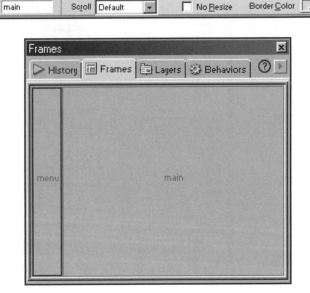

Open the <u>Frames</u> tab. The preview window reflects the setup of your frames. Click on a frame to select it. You cannot modify the position of your frames from within this window, only select them. When you have selected a frame, the <u>Frames Properties Inspector</u> will present you with further options concerning your chosen frame.

In the <u>Frame Name</u> field of the <u>Properties Inspector</u>, enter a name for your frame. This name must be unique and, if possible, relevant to the content of the frame (for example, if you are going to use a left frame for a menu bar, it is perfectly OK to call it "menu"). The <u>Scroll</u> dropdown menu is used to determine whether or not the frame will have a scrolling bar attached to it, and if so, how it is will behave (see below). Use the <u>Src</u> field to tell the frame which page it will display when someone accesses the site. You can either enter an address here or you can select a URL by using the folder icon.

There are four options for you to choose from as far as scrolling is concerned. You can select one of the options for each of your frames. They are as follows:

Yes: If you select this, a scroll bar will be attached to the right-hand side and the bottom of your frame.

No: Your frame will never have a scrollbar. This is perfect if the content of the frame is definitely not going to change (for example, if it is a fixed menu). However, if you will be changing the pages in that frame and they may be of varying sizes, you may lose information if you have no scrolling.

Auto: In this instance, a scroll bar will automatically appear if one is needed. For example, if your visitor resizes their web browser window or if you have a very large page, the browser will automatically start to scroll to the right and below the frame as necessary.

Default: Whether or not you have scroll bars will be determined by your visitor's web browser.

TO SCROLL OR NOT TO SCROLL?

Scroll bars can look bulky and unattractive. If you are sure that you don't need any, for instance if your menu is small and would require your visitor to view your page in a tiny window to hide any information in the menu frame, it is quite safe to turn the scroll bar off. In any doubt, use the <u>Auto</u> setting and do it the easy way: let someone else decide for you.

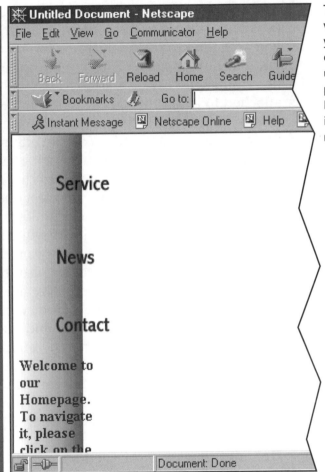

This is an example of what will happen if you set the scrolling option to <u>No</u> and an unexpectedly large page is loaded. Important information is missing.

DISPLAYING PAGES IN A FRAME

When you set up a frameset, you also need to tell each frame what to display. If you don't, the frameset will look for a non-existent file and will display an error message. Each frame must have a page to display in it. This is set up by using the <u>Src</u> option in the <u>Properties Inspector</u> when your frame is selected.

Tell each frame to display a particular HTML file by entering the address or selecting the file.

TARGETING A FRAME

Now that your frameset is set up, you will also need to set up the links in the rest of your site to reflect them. This leads to the introduction of a new term: target. Each hyperlink you build in your web pages can target a particular frame, if necessary. Targeting a frame means that you tell the hyperlink to point not only to a given file, but also to the frame that displays it. You have already built hyperlinks. Click on the text or the image you want to use as a link and go to the <u>Text</u> (or <u>Image</u>) <u>Properties Inspector</u>. Fill in your link as normal, in the <u>Link</u> field. Next to it is the <u>Target</u> field. In here you should enter the name of the frame you wish the hyperlink to be displayed in.

Create a hyperlink and target the frame to display. Then specify the name of the frame you want to display it in in the <u>Target</u> box.

Here is an example. Say you have a frameset made of two vertical frames: "menu" on the left and "main" on the right. In the "menu" frame is a series of buttons that link to "Sales", "Products" and "Contact" web pages. All you have to do to set this up properly is to create your links for each web page with the relevant item in the menu ("Sales" linking to "sales.html", "contact" linking to "contact.html" etc.) and set the <u>Target</u> for each link as "main". All the web pages (sales.html, contact.html etc.) that are selected from the menu situated in the left (menu) frame will be displayed in the right (main) frame. This is shown below.

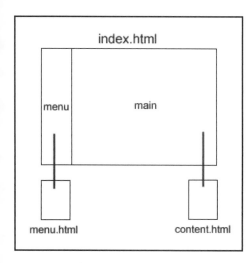

The links from the left frame will be displayed in the right frame.

USES OF FRAMES

Frames are useful as soon as you have a page with elements in it that you know will not change. An attractive way of using frames is to put backgrounds behind them. An example of this is shown below. You can build a special web page with a logo on it and set it as a frame so that it will always be visible wherever your visitor ends up in your site. You can also add frames within frames (this is called nesting).

1 Create a whole page with this kind of graded image as a tiled background.

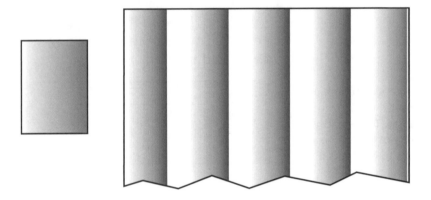

2 Place the page in a frame on the left-hand side of your browser window. (In this case the frame was expanded to the right, so that some of the white in the tiled image showed through).

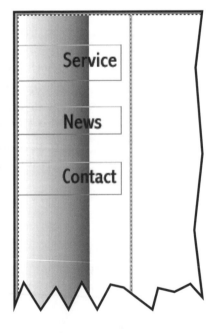

Service

News

Contact

Contact

3 Place your menu items in layers over the top of the framed page for a more interesting and original menu.

NESTING FRAMES

To add frames into other frames, simply select your original starting frame and click on the type of frame you want inside it from the list in the <u>Objects</u> palette.

Some elements in a web page – a logo or an address, for example – need to be always visible. Place them in a frame inside a frameset.

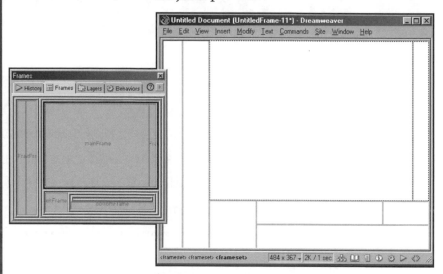

CALLING FRAMESETS FROM WITHIN A FRAMESET

Things can get pretty complicated when you call framesets from within other framesets. This could happen, for instance, if you have a menu for your site and each item in the menu triggers a submenu. A simple example that springs to mind is that of a multilingual site. You can have the whole site written three times (e.g. in English, French and Spanish), with the corresponding menus, and a bigger main menu to allow your visitor to switch from one language to another. Images of flags (for instance) in the first frameset will have hyperlinks targeting the frame named "main". The items in the submenus link to the frame "submenu" will target the frame called "content".

FRAMES AND EXTERNAL LINKS

You will have to be careful about frames when you create external links. If you point to a web site somebody else built, you might end up with their frames all over your site. Always check the way your external links behave: you are in control of your work, but not that of others.

WORKING WITH ROLLOVERS

If you browse the Web, the chances are that you have seen a lot of rollovers. They are images that change when your mouse "rolls" over them. Rollovers are fairly easy to set up and can add an extra touch to your site. Rollovers will also add functionality, especially when they are placed in a menu – even more if your menu is in a frame.

To create rollovers you must first understand a bit about how your mouse works in a browser. Your mouse has two buttons, left and right. Each action performed by the left button results in what we (and a web browser) will call a "state". There are two basic states: Down, which occurs when the button is pressed, and Up, when it is released. Two other states are Over, which occurs when your mouse is place over an area, and Out, when it leaves a particular area. Rollovers check the position and state of your mouse and react depending on what they find. To create a rollover, you will need at least two images: one image – the primary image – as a base, for the latent state (when nothing happens or when the mouse goes Out of the rollover). The other image – the rollover – is the one that will be displayed when your mouse rolls over the first image (hence the name).

1 The first step when creating a rollover is to create two images. Each will match a "state" of the mouse.

2 When you have highlighted your image, select <u>Swap Image</u> from the list of actions in the <u>Behaviors</u> tab. You will be presented with the <u>Swap Image</u> dialog box. You will need to assign an Action to your <u>Swap Image</u> Event. The most common one is <u>onMouseOver</u>.

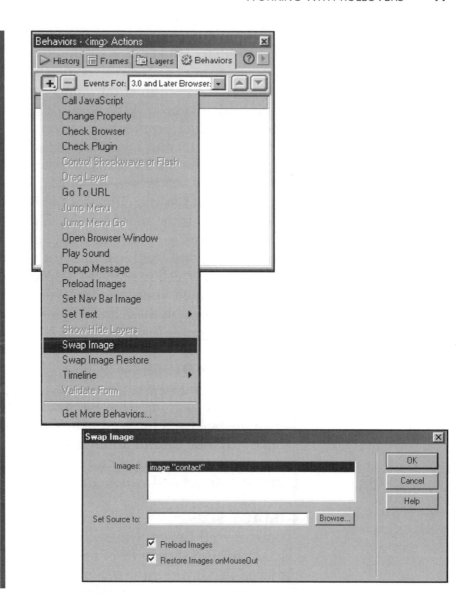

3 All you have to do to create your rollover is simply enter the path to your second image file. The <u>Images</u> field will list all the images you currently have in your web page. Use the <u>Set Source to</u> box to browse for your second image. This is the one that will be displayed when your mouse goes over the first one. Leave the <u>Preload Images</u> button ticked and both of the images will load with the rest of the page, rather than your browser having to wait until the mouse goes over the image to access it. This will make the page a tiny bit slower to load, but give it a quicker feel. Tick the <u>Restore Images onMouseOut</u> box to make sure that your first image is displayed again when your mouse goes out of the second image.

ASSIGNING IMAGES

The easiest way to build a rollover is by using the <u>Swap Image</u> option in the <u>Behaviors</u> tab. Bring up the <u>Behaviors</u> tab by typing <u>F8</u> or choose <u>WINDOW/BEHAVIORS</u> in the main menu bar. Click on the image you want to start with (the primary image) and then on the <u>+</u> sign toward the top of the <u>Behaviors</u> tab to bring down the list of actions you can assign to it.

As you can see, the names of the images listed are not their file names. It is the name you have given them when you first inserted them into your page. If you do not give any names to your images, you will end up with a list of "unnamed image number X", which is not very helpful, to say the least. If you have not named your images, layers and tables properly, do so now. Just click on them and fill in the <u>Image Name</u> box in the <u>Image Properties Inspector</u>.

SWAPPING OTHER IMAGES

You can, if you so wish, change an image other than the one your mouse is going over. Simply specify another image name than the one used for your primary image in the Swap Images dialog box. Be careful, though – things can get confusing at this point, as you might find it difficult to remember which image changes and which image triggered this change.

IMAGE SIZE

Both of your images (the source image and the image that it changes into) should be of identical size, especially if they are placed in a layer. If the second image is larger than the first, the layer will automatically resize it, but this may cause strange effects.

THE FIRST PAGE   _ ⧉ ✕

By convention, a web browser will look for a file called index.html when it first reaches a site. If you want to start your site with your frameset, the set will have to be called index.html. If you have upgraded your site from a non-frame version, your old index.html will need to have a different name. A good choice is intro.html.

TRIGGERING A ROLLOVER WITH ANOTHER ACTION

OnMouseOver is the most common instruction to trigger a rollover. You can choose to swap your image if your visitor performs another action, though, such as a double-click of the mouse or a combination of a mouse click and a keystroke. To do this, set up a rollover as described above, then click on the OnMouseOver action in the Behaviors tab and then on the down arrow next to it.

From the dropdown list, pick the Action you want to assign to your image swapping operation.
onMouseDown will only trigger an image swap if the viewer clicks on the left mouse button while their mouse is on the image. This creates a more traditional button that the user has to click on.

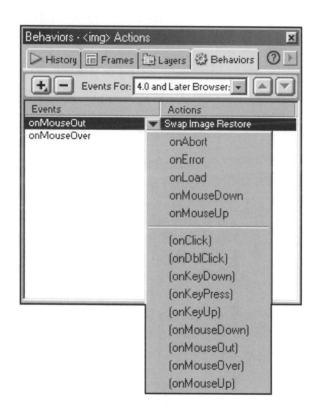

SWAPPING TWO IMAGES AT THE SAME TIME

Some web site-building programs such as Adobe GoLive 4 offer you the option to swap two images at the same time. This is an improvement, but such operations can only be understood by certain types of web browsers (namely IE 4 and 5). If you are building a site specifically for these web browsers, fine. If not, keep to the old-fashioned single image swap.

ANIMATING WITH THE TIMELINE

Animated GIF images are only one of various ways to have animated graphics in your site. In Dreamweaver you have another option, called the Timeline. Most major web design packages have a feature like this and, used effectively, it can create some stunning effects.

With the Timeline you select a layer (and therefore its contents) and give it a starting and a finishing position. The starting position is where the layer will be at the beginning of the animation and the finishing position is – well, where the layer will end up at the end of the animation. The starting and finishing positions are defined by you in the <u>Timelines</u> tab. So, to create a simple Timeline animation, you will need to start with two things: a layer that you want to animate and the <u>Timelines</u> tab. The Timelines tab is accessed with the keyboard shortcut <u>Ctrl+F9</u>, or you can choose <u>WINDOW/TIMELINE</u> from the main menu bar to summon it to your desktop.

1 Bring up the <u>Timelines Inspector</u>. The vertical numbers on the bar represent the layers of the Timeline – you can use the Timeline to animate more than one object in your web page using this feature. Name your Timeline.

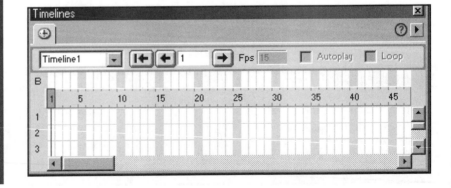

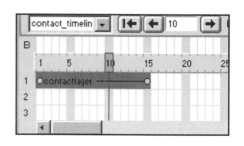

2 Select the layer that you want to animate. It should contain an image or some text. Drag it on to one of the layers in the Timeline. The name of the layer will appear in a darkened line. The line will have a fat white dot at each end of it. These dots are key frames.

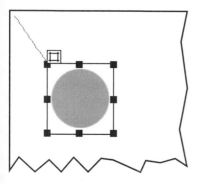

3 Drag your layer to the position you want it to start in the animation. Click on the last key point on that layer's line in the <u>Timelines Inspector</u>. Then click on your layer and drag it to the position you want it to be in at the end of the animation. Dreamweaver will automatically calculate the position of your layer for each frame. A coloured line will appear to show you the path the layer will use to move in your page.

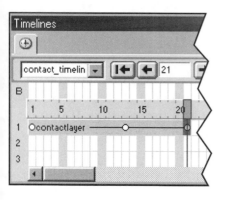

4 The cells (called frames) that contain a fat white dot are key frames. They show specific steps in an animation and you can add key frames to your animation if you want to change its direction. If you need your animation to be longer or shorter than the default 15 frames, click on the last key frame and drag it left or right.

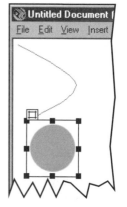

5 Repeat the previous steps and add key frames (Ctrl+Click in a frame makes it a key frame) to get the perfect path for your animation.

Each layer in your page can be added to the Timeline and animated.

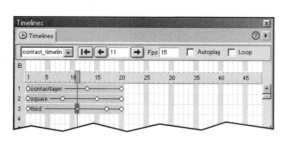

MOVING AROUND IN CIRCLES

You are not confined to up, down, left or right movements for your animations. If you want your layer to move on a curve, all you have to do is to add a key frame. Ctrl-click anywhere inside your Timeline layer: a key frame will appear. Change its position to the frame you want and drag your object layer to a suitable intermediate position. The line describing the path of your animation will change to a curve. To select a key frame, simply click on it.

MULTIPLE TIMELINES

You can animate more than one element in your page. All you have to do is drag the layer you wish to animate into another layer in the Timelines tab and modify it as explained above. To select a Timeline layer just click on it. Note, though, that all the frames between key frames are "frozen": their state cannot be changed. If you click on a single frame in the Timeline and drag your object layer around, it will modify the whole Timeline, not the behaviour of that particular frame.

AUTOPLAY

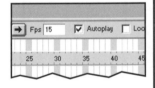

The Autoplay tick box. Select this to automatically play your animations.

To start your animation as soon as the web page that it is in loads, you will need to instruct Dreamweaver to do this. The Autoplay box in the Timelines tab will do just that. If you do not tick this box, your web browser will wait for a particular event (for example the mouse passing over a particular point or a button being clicked on) to happen before starting the animation.

TRIGGERING THE ANIMATION

If you do not want to Autoplay the animation, you will need to choose under which circumstances to play it – the Event that you want to associate with the Action of playing your animation. This is done through the Behaviors Inspector in a way we have looked at before (for swapping images). First, select the image that will trigger the animation. Then bring up the Behaviors tab (F8), click on the ± symbol and go down to Timeline in the popdown menu.

1 Using the <u>Behaviors</u> tab, select what you want to do with your Timeline animation: go to a certain frame, Play or Stop. The <u>Play Timeline</u> and <u>Stop Timeline</u> Actions are self-explanatory. You may not wish to play the whole animation, though, and this is where the <u>Go To Timeline Frame</u> option comes in handy – you can select the point in the Timeline at which your animation will start.

2 Select the relevant Timeline when you have chosen your Action.

3 The <u>Go To Timeline Frame</u> dialog box will appear if you selected <u>Go To Timeline Frame</u>. Enter the number of the frame you want the animation to jump to in the <u>Go to Frame</u> box when you have selected the Timeline you need to use from the dropdown list. Then, using the <u>Loop</u> box, select how many times you wish the animation to repeat itself (if you want it to).

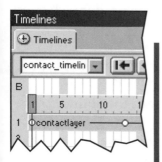

1 Click on the desired frame in the <u>Behavior Channel</u> to select it.

ADD AN ACTION TO A KEY FRAME

Each frame in an animation can trigger an action. You can, for example, swap one image for another or play a sound every time your animation reaches a certain frame. This introduces the <u>Behavior Channel</u>, found above the frame numbers in the Timeline window and marked with a "B".

You cannot modify the Event for this Action in the <u>Behaviors</u> tab (the Action is always triggered when you reach the frame you selected) but you can add Actions in the same ways as before. You can trigger any kind of Action you want (change some text, bring up a window, play a sound etc.), but they must always be started with an "onFrame" command. This will be the frame you selected in the Behavior Channel.

ADDING SOUND TO YOUR PAGES

We have already looked at animation, image-swapping and frames. There is one more key effect that can enhance the impact of your web pages – sound effects. Adding a couple of subtle sounds to key parts of your site can make all the difference.

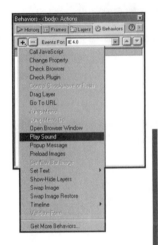

1 Select <u>Play Sound</u> from the <u>Behaviors</u> tab.

2 Select the sound file to use in the <u>Play Sound</u> dialog box.

To play a sound in your web page, you will need to "attach" it to an action such as the passage of the mouse over a picture, or when the page loads. So, as you've seen before, you will need the <u>Behaviors</u> tab. Hit the <u>F8</u> key on your keyboard to bring it up if it is not already visible on your desktop. How do you start the music or a sound playing? Select an image, some text or any other element that can trigger an action (even a frame in a Timeline). When you have chosen an item, click on the <u>+</u> sign in the <u>Behaviors</u> tab and select <u>Play Sound</u>.

In the <u>Play Sound</u> dialog box that appears, browse for the sound file you wish to use or type its path in the <u>Play Sound</u> field.

That's all there is to it. If you do not want the sound to play when the page loads (denoted by <u>onLoad</u> in the <u>Events</u> list), go back to the <u>Behaviors</u> tab and check out a few additional options by clicking on the down arrow that will have appeared in the <u>Event</u> menu. This is what your options will be:

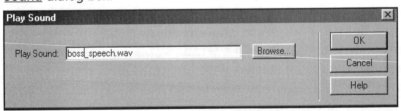

3 More actions are available to you when you opt to play your sound when the page is being loaded.

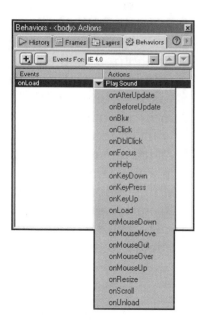

onBlur: this happens when an action stops being the focus of the user's attention. For instance, if they have typed in some information in a text field and then clicked outside it (to register it).

onError: this plays the sound when an error of any kind happens as the page is being loaded.

onFocus: this is the opposite of OnBlur. The sound will play when the user begins to use a certain object.

onLoad: the action will be triggered when the web page is being loaded.

onResize: this will play the sound when the page's window is resized.

onUnload: the sound will play when your visitor leaves the page.

If you do not find the action you need in the list, try changing the web browser specification in the Events For list in the Behaviors tab. Your sound-triggering Event may be limited by the browser limitations you have specified. Remember, you can assign these Actions to any elements you want to incorporate in your pages, not just sounds.

SOUND FORMATS

The basic file format for web sound is called WAV and is symbolized by the extension .wav. These files can be easily read by any web browser on any machine, be they Windows-based systems or Macintosh. The only problem with this file format is that it can generate pretty big files. There is no way you can record your musical creation in WAV format and distribute it on the Web: a one-minute sound file will end up as approximately 10 megabytes! Therefore, it is better to use simple, short sounds in your pages. Windows' Sound Recorder and a microphone are all you need to record a short message or a noise. With Sound Recorder, you can set the quality of the sound and add effects. Experiment and compromise – you don't need CD quality for most sounds.

Windows' Media Recorder. A very useful, no nonsense sound program ideal for the web.

There are many other formats available for the web, but they have a drawback: most of them will require a plugin. Here is an introduction to playing sounds on your pages with them.

   The RealAudio plugin can be found at http://www.realaudio.com. Grab it from there and install it on your own machine. RealAudio provides streaming music and sound, which means that as it reads a sound file it places some of it in a buffer (a portion of your computer's memory or a temporary folder) and stores it there at the same time as playing the start of it. As the buffer empties, RealAudio refills it with the buffer mentioned above. This is a smart way of keeping your visitor interested in your sounds, despite long download times.

RealAudio is the most popular plugin for music and sounds.

Here is the RealAudio player in action.

You will have to tell your viewer that the file he or she wants to load requires a plugin. It is not very good form, therefore, to start a RealAudio file immediately as the page loads: your viewer might not wish (or might not be able to) install a plugin or external program on their system. Adding a small logo as a trigger for the file will solve this problem.

Add a graphic to warn your visitors that they need a plugin to hear the music or sound. Use the image to link to the plugin's download page.

Most plugins come with their own instructions, available online, and will tell you how to insert a hyperlink from your site to their own download site. This makes things easy for your visitors.

.MID FILES

There is another useful format available for the web: .MID files. These files play a simple type of music that you may recognize as similar to old computer games. Another choice that you have is to add small programs – available for free on the web – to play sounds. If you are aiming high, Macromedia Flash 4 – a hybrid piece of web/graphic design software – can deal with the famous .MP3 files. MP3s can compress music to near-CD quality in ten times less file size than a compact disc.

CHECKING YOUR SITE

In the same way that you should save your work regularly and back everything up at the end of your working day, it is imperative that you check the behaviour of your site before making it available for others to see.

Checking your site is vital. It can't be stressed enough. Other people from all over the world will be accessing your site and you should be prepared for as many different situations as possible: fast machines, slow machines, black-and-white monitors, IBM-compatibles, Mac-compatibles and so on. Fortunately, you do not have to check your site online all the time. You can easily check it first on your own computer and then, if everything is OK and you have uploaded it to where it is supposed to be on the World Wide Web, check it once again online.

It is best to use the spellchecker, even if you checked your text before importing it.

THE SPELLCHECKER

The first thing to look for in your site are typos (typographic mistakes). If you used a word processor to type your text and then cut and pasted it into your page, this operation may not be required as you will probably have had the text spellchecked in the word editor itself. If this is not the case, Dreamweaver (as well as all major web design programs) has a built-in spellchecker called up by using the key combination <u>Ctrl+F7</u> (or <u>TEXT/CHECK SPELLING</u> in the main menu bar).

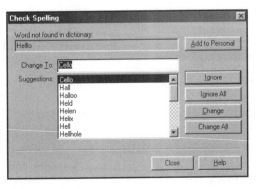

If the spellchecker finds any mistakes, correct them using the proper word in the <u>Suggestions</u> list or by filling in your own correction and then click on the <u>Change</u> or <u>Change All</u> buttons, which will change either that instance of the word or all instances of that word, respectively. Once the spellcheck is complete, check your images. If there is any text in them, is it correctly spelled? Are the right images in the right places? Is everything right with the size and the colour?

CHECKING LINKS

The <u>Check Links Sitewide</u> option will check all the hyperlinks on your site for you to make sure that they are working properly. If anything is wrong, it is up to you to rectify the problem because Dreamweaver 3 cannot guess which links are meant to go where by itself. If there is a mistake you have make across the whole site, you can use the option <u>Change Links Sitewide</u> (<u>SITE/CHANGE LINKS SITEWIDE</u>) to modify all the instances of a particular hyperlink. You will find a <u>Replace What</u> field (choose the hyperlink you want to replace) and a <u>By What</u> field (choose which file the new link will point to). By clicking on the down arrow in the <u>Show</u> list, you can select what to check: the internal or external links (you will need to be connected to the web for the latter) and also the orphan files. An orphan file is a file that doesn't have any incoming link, which means that there isn't a page in your site that points to it.

PREVIEW IN LOCAL BROWSER

The next step will be to check how your site behaves in a web browser. Some elements, such as Timelines for instance, cannot be checked in Dreamweaver 3 alone.

Select what you want to check in the Show field. All the files with problems will be listed in the dropdown menu.

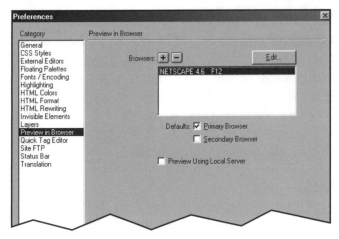

When you are checking your site in a browser you will need to tell Dreamweaver 3 which web browser to use to check the integrity of your whole site. Choose Preview in Browser… in the FILE section of the main menu. If this section is empty, you will need to define your list of web browsers. FILE/PREVIEW IN BROWSER/EDIT BROWSER LIST will bring up the Preferences dialog box. Click on Preview in Browser from the menu on the left.

Define the web browsers you wish to use to check your site for errors. Use the ± sign to add a browser and the - sign to remove it from the list. Determine which will be your primary and secondary browser with the Primary and Secondary buttons.

When you click on the ± sign, a dialog box will pop up asking you to give a name to your new browser and where to find it. If you are not satisfied with your settings, click the Edit button to edit the specifications of your web browser.

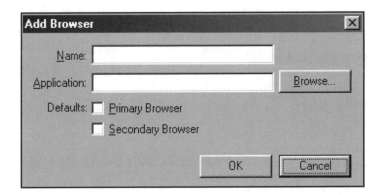

The Add Browser dialog box.

Once a primary browser has been defined, open your home page (usually index.html). Press F12. Your primary browser will launch with your home page in it. From then on, check everything: the links, the images, popup windows, sounds, animation etc. Correct any mistakes and make sure that your site works exactly the way you designed it to.

INTERACTIVITY

5

Having your visitor email you straight from your site is a good way to add interactivity. It is limited, though – you have no control over the content of the message itself. It may contain information you don't need or omit vital details that you do. To make sure that you know what you will be getting, use forms. You probably receive at least one to fill in every day through the post, so you know what forms are and what they are for. Imagine the same thing online and you are ready to set up your own.

CGI

CGI stands for Common Gateway Interface. It is a way of processing and transferring information from a web page to you. CGI is used to build scripts (most of the time you will hear the expression "CGI script" when talking about CGI). The scripts are executable programs that reside on your web server's hard disk. Your visitor sends information to the server and this information is processed and sent back to you (or you can arrange for the information to be sent to others).

These scripts can be written in a variety of programming languages, but you won't have to learn any of these languages to make use of CGI scripts. Most ISPs will be happy to accept CGI scripts that you have written, if you have any, and they will set them up for you. CGI scripts are accessed via the web and usually through a form.

WHAT IS A FORM?

Forms are special web pages that instruct your web browser to go to a CGI script (on a server) and process some data. The CGI script is, in most cases, a form-to-mail script: that is, a CGI program that will collect the data entered by your visitor and send it to you in a clear, organized and readable way via email. It is this kind of script you are going to see an example of in this book. For security reasons (after all, a CGI script is a program and you don't want just anyone to run any kind of program on your own computer), CGI scripts are kept in a special folder by your ISP and their access is restricted to a specific type of use.

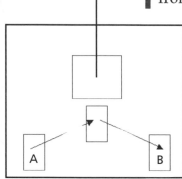

The CGI script on the web server processes the form.

There are a lot of CGI scripts around, but the one you are most likely to use initially (and the one that we will explore in this chapter) is called "formmail.cgi". This file is available free from the web or you can probably get a copy from your ISP.

When you get it, have a look at it using a text editor (Microsoft WordPad or Apple SimpleText). If you have any programming experience, you might see roughly how it works. If not, you can probably guess some of the instructions that are passed from the form to the email. If you are into that sort of thing, you can even write your own scripts and ask your ISP to activate them.

FORM-TO-EMAIL CGI SCRIPTS

The form you built (A) is viewed and completed by someone on the web. The result of this processing is sent to you via email (B).

When you use formmail.cgi you will need to create a form for your visitor to fill in. The form will send the relevant information to the CGI script for processing. The CGI script will process this information, check it for consistency and then send you back the results to you via email.

As you can see in the above illustration, the email you get is pretty thorough and to the point. Only the information you need will be sent. You can set up your forms so that each is sent to a different recipient (requests for service to the aftersales department, requests for technical support to the technical support department and so forth). As with any email, the feedback will reach you very quickly, depending on your ISP's performance, making forms a very useful tool to feature in your site.

The email returned to you from a form you created, posted by somebody, somewhere, browsing your site.

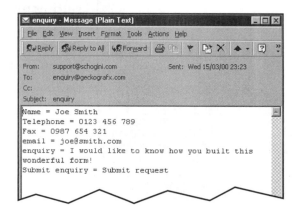

SETTING UP A FORM

A form on your site can help you in many ways. It can contain the fields to enter the information you specifically need and nothing else. Be it a request for service, a personal database of contacts or a quote, you will get exactly what you need from your visitor.

GENERAL ENQUIRIES

Please use this form to contact us. All information given will be treated with strict confidentiality.

General enquiries

Name (first and last)

Telephone

Fax

E mail

Enquiry

Form complete   Submit request   Reset

GeckoGrafx

HELP
Forms can become complicated and you will almost definitely need some help from your ISP in order to set them up. Check out their home pages, email them or phone them up and tell them you want to set up forms on your site. They will provide you with the path(s) to the CGI script(s) you want to use. Write down this path and keep it safe, as it is a vital part of setting up your forms. Your ISP might also give you additional advice and information, such as the fields you can use in your form.

An example of a professional form. A user will imput their details and simply click on Submit request to send the information to you. As far as the user is concerned, there is no email involved.

SETTING UP A FORM

Forms can be pretty straightforward to set up. All the major web design programs will offer to build forms for you. You insert elements in a form the same way that you insert pictures and text: by using a collection of icons on the <u>Forms</u> palette. Forms are made of form elements, which can be found in the <u>Objects</u> palette if you click on the down arrow at the top of it and select <u>Forms</u> from the list.

FORM ELEMENTS

Here is a list of the various forms elements you can add to your site.

Form: this is the core – the form itself. All of the other elements will need to be placed **inside** the form.

Text Field: this is where your visitor will input some text.

Insert Button: this icon will insert a button to submit or reset the form.

Check Box: your visitor can select multiple check boxes if they wish.

Radio Button: unlike check boxes, when you click on a radio button you will uncheck all the other radio buttons in the group (to belong to a group, radio buttons must have the same name).

List/Menu: either gives a popup list of entries (you can only select one of them) or a menu list (you can select more than one option).

File Field: will allow your visitor to upload files to your web site.

Image Field: use this instead of a button to submit a form or perform an action.

Hidden Field: this icon represents a field that does not require any information to be input from your visitor but that will still be processed by the CGI script.

Jump Menu: this will let you create a menu with hyperlinks to different files.

The <u>Forms</u> elements in the <u>Objects</u> palette. If you can't see all of the palette, click on the arrow pointing down on the bottom left.

FIRST STEP

Your first step will be to create a new document by pressing Ctrl+N. Click in the new blank page and then click on the Insert Form icon in the Forms palette. A red dotted rectangle shows the form in your page.

1 Insert a form in your new page. All the form elements you will add will have to be added within the boundaries of this rectangle. If you try to place an element outside this form, Dreamweaver will assume you are starting another form and ask if you want to add another form (by using a form tag).

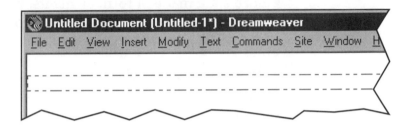

Now turn your attention to the Form Properties Inspector. Before you do anything else, give your form a name. The name must start with a letter and be unique. The default "method" (a description of what the form does) is set by Dreamweaver 3 to Post. Leave it like that, because you are going to post information from your page to the CGI script. In the Action box, type in the path to your CGI directory, as supplied to you by your ISP. This is the critical information you need to set up a successful form.

2 Modify the fields in the Form Properties Inspector according to your needs. Enter the path of the CGI script in the Action box you are going to use – this will have been supplied by your ISP.

ADDING ELEMENTS

Now that your form has been started, you can add form elements to it. You cannot place these elements in layers because they need to be inside the form itself – inside the dotted rectangle. So click inside your form and then on the element you need in the Forms palette. First of all, we'll look at what happens when you add a Text Field.

THE TEXT FIELD

This is where your visitor will enter some text; for a description, a comment, an address, etc. Each time you add a form element, the <u>Properties Inspector</u> will change to display the properties of this element.

3 Start adding form elements. In this example, a text field.

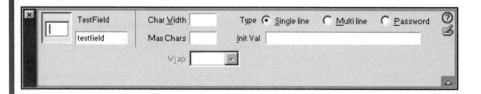

Name: as always, to avoid any confusion, name your field, especially if you need more than one.

Char Width: this box will specify how wide your text field will be (the number of characters it will accommodate in one line). Guess the probable length of the information you require in this field and modify the value accordingly.

Max Char: specify the maximum number of characters your visitor will be allowed to type. Use this, for instance, when you need a postal code or a password containing no more than a limited number of characters to be entered in this field.

Init Val: anything typed in this box will appear as text in the text field when the form is loaded. It will be superseded by your visitor's own input text.

Multi line: if the information that has to be entered is likely to be long, convert a single-line text box into a multi-line one.

Wrap: this option will be active only if you insert a multi-line text box. Keep this as Default to let the web browser determine how to handle the way the text will wrap inside the text field.

Password: the Password radio button will scramble the text typed and your visitor will only see a string of dots.

NAMING CONVENTIONS

Each name for your form elements must start with a letter and be unique, even if the same elements are placed in different forms within your site.

CHECK BOXES AND RADIO BUTTONS

Each of these two components will be either on or off. If they are off (unchecked), the returned result (when the form has been processed) will be nil. If they are on (checked), the returned result will be whatever you put in the <u>Checked Value</u> field. If two radio buttons have the same name, they will belong to the same group. If you then check one button, the other buttons in the group will become unchecked. Apart from that, they work the same way as check boxes.

The <u>Checkbox Properties Inspector</u> window. You can decide which state the box will be in (checked or unchecked) when the page starts loading.

Here is an example: you might need to know whether your visitor agrees to let you use their details to send them a catalog. Place the checkbox in your form and set the name to "Catalog" and the <u>Checked Value</u> to "Yes". If your visitor checks this box, your email will read "Catalog: Yes". If not, it will read only "Catalog:" and a blank line.

LIST AND MENU FIELDS

The same icon serves two purposes: creating a dropdown menu or a list. You will have the option of choosing between the two by going to the <u>List/Menu Properties Inspector</u> window. A menu or a list needs two sets of information: a description and a value that the description relates to. You define values for your menu or list by clicking the <u>List Values</u> button in the <u>Menu/List Properties Inspector</u>. Your visitor will only see the description, while the value attached to it when they select an item will be returned to you via email when the form is processed.

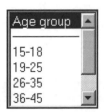

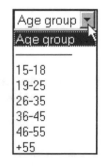

Give your visitor a menu (above) or a list (right) to choose the information they need.

Only the description (not the value) will be visible in your menu or your list field. In this below, the form asks the viewer which age group he or she belongs to. Each option you give has a corresponding value. When your visitor chooses an item in the list, the relevant value will be processed by the CGI script. Follow the example below and name your list or menu, say, "Age group". The email you will receive will read: "Age group: 15 to 18" (depending on your visitor's answer). The main difference between a menu and a list, apart from their appearance, is that a list will allow multiple selection: more than one item can be chosen from the list at the same time.

Choose to build a list which will enable the visitor to select more than one entry by clicking on the <u>Allow Multiple</u> button.

When you work with a list, you can define which item will be already ticked when the page is loaded by selecting <u>Initially Selected</u> in the <u>Menu/List Inspector</u>. Other options include: **Height**: when creating a list, you can specify the number of items visible to start with. All the other items will require your

Click on the <u>List Values</u> button in the <u>Menu/List Inspector</u>. List the values to go in your menu or your list in the <u>List Values</u> dialog box.

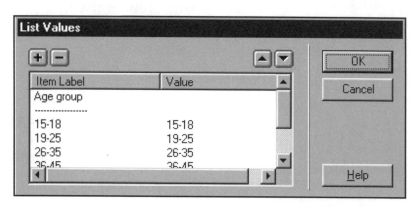

visitor to use the scrollbar to see them.

+ and – sign: click on the + sign to add an entry. Click an entry and then on the - sign to remove it from the list.

Label: enter a description for the entry.

Value: enter the value for this entry.

Arrows: click one of the arrows to move an item up or down in the list (click on the given item to select it first).

Although you cannot test the actual working of your form offline when you use a form-to-mail CGI script (because the script is on your ISP's server), you can still check how the various components work. Press F12 and run your form in the web browser you have defined as your primary web browser. When you click on the first entry in a menu, a dropdown menu should appear with all your descriptions in it.

The Value for an item can be anything. If the menu or list is part of a form that will send you back an email, the entries in it can be names of products, the age of the visitor, the country they live in etc. In the case of a menu, you can assign a hyperlink to each entry. This is a slightly different use of forms, but still deals with your user's input. When your viewer selects an entry, they will automatically be sent to the relevant page. This is an alternative – or a complement – to a menu in a frame, although you might wish to use a Jump Menu instead. When you use a menu this way, you do not need to insert it into a form because the action it performs will not be processed by a script, but by the web browser itself.

1 The Insert Jump Menu icon in the Forms palette. While you can use a standard menu to create hyperlinks within each entry, a Jump Menu contains additional options, such as specifying a target for your hyperlink, to control the operation better.

All the entries in your Jump Menu will be visible here.

Enter some text to describe the link this entry points to. Click on the + sign to add more entries and on the - sign to delete them.

Specify where this link is going by either typing in a URL or browse for an HTML file.

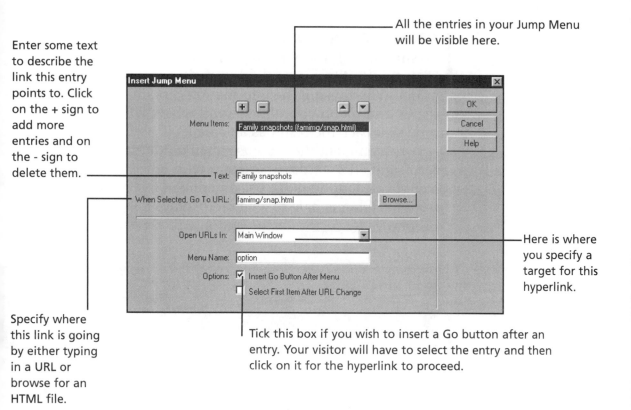

Here is where you specify a target for this hyperlink.

Tick this box if you wish to insert a Go button after an entry. Your visitor will have to select the entry and then click on it for the hyperlink to proceed.

JUMP MENU

Once the Jump Menu is set up, click on it to select it and go back to the Properties Inspector. It looks just like a standard menu, and can be edited the same way but for one thing: you can specify a target. If you don't need a target, use a Jump Menu instead of a standard menu.

It is also good idea to use a similar Jump Menu across your site so that the navigation remains the same, unless you just want to use it as a one-off for a specific series of pages that can be accessed only through this particular page.

DOTTED LINE SEPARATORS   _ 🗗 ✕

You can arrange your entries into sections by using a separator: instead of typing a description in the entry field, type a line of dots (or hyphens or stars) and leave the When Selected field blank.

SUBMIT YOUR FORM

To submit your form, the easiest way is to add a Submit button to it. When your send-to-mail form is complete, this button will transmit the information contained in the page to the CGI script on your web server, which will process it and send you back the result as an email.

We recomment that you use a Submit button for your first form, and afterwards experiment with other, more complicated, options. To use a plain Submit button, insert it from the Objects palette when it displays Forms objects. The Properties Inspector for the button will appear as follows:

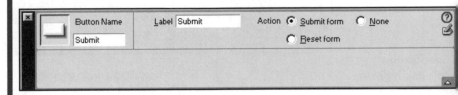

Name: as for all other components of your web page, this button will need to be named.

Label: The convention is to leave this field as Submit.

Action: select what this button will do. Submit the form (send it to be processed by the CGI script), Reset it (all the information entered in the form will be erased) or None.

The submit button will work with the attributes you have specified for your form, as explained previously. What it will do is send the form to the Action address that you set earlier (page 96). It is for this reason that the Action address is so important, and this is why a form cannot function properly if the address is misspelled or wrong. Remember to contact your ISP or go to their web page for this address.

Send your form to be processed with a button that will
usually look like this – Dreamweaver's default Submit button.

HIDDEN FIELDS

Hidden fields are fields that do not require any input from your visitor, but that can still be processed by the CGI script you are using with this form. As the name implies, they will not appear in the web browser but will work in the background. Some of them, however, are essential to your form and cannot be omitted. Others are optional. ISPs do not all work with the same form-to-mail scripts. Some of the hidden fields given here might not work as they are and may need to be slightly modified, although the basic process will remain the same. You should be given information on hidden fields when you are supplied with details about CGI scripts in general by your ISP.

1 Click inside your form, select the Hidden Field button and check out the Hidden Field Properties Inspector. Note the Parameter box and the Value box.

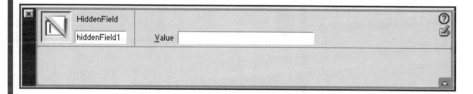

All hidden fields require two pieces of information: a Parameter and a Value. The Parameter will be interpreted by the CGI script as a variable integrated in its code; for instance something like, "if X= this Parameter then perform the Value Y." The Parameter you specify in the hidden field will be X and, depending on what it is, the action declared in Value will be triggered. A bit confusing? Let's have a look at an example.

When sending a form while browsing the web, you submit the form and then get redirected to a page saying "Thank you for your comment; it will be processed as soon as possible". This is done with a hidden field placed in the form you just filled in. The chances are that the Parameter for this hidden field was THANKSURL and that the Value was the actual URL of the Thank You page created by the designers of the site. The word THANKSURL, when received by the CGI script, was interpreted as an instruction to display the page at the URL specified in the Value.

USING HIDDEN FIELDS

Depending on the form-to-mail program your ISP uses, you will be able to get different information. One thing that must be part of your form, and that has not been covered yet, is where to send the results of a form. You do this by adding a hidden field, usually labelled RECIPIENT, in which the Value is your email address (it is placed in a hidden field because you might not want your visitor to know where the form is going). To place a hidden field you just select one from the Objects palette and place it in the form. To make it an email reply address you label it RECIPIENT and add your email address as the value.

2 Specify where the result of the CGI processing of your form is going to go.

Another hidden field available to you is the NOBLANK parameter. Type this in the Parameter (name) box in the Properties Inspector and the name of the text box you want filled in in the Value box. This will tell the CGI script to check whether something has been typed in the text box you specified. If the text box has something in it, the CGI script will carry on as normal. If not, your visitor will be redirected to a new page saying, for example, "Sorry, but it seems you forgot to fill in your postal code, this information is essential". They will then be taken back to the original form. This is useful when you want the user to enter a specific piece of information, such as a reply address or an email address.

Other hidden fields include the possibility of knowing which web browser your visitor uses or the date the form was sent. You can even ask your CGI script to check whether an email address has been correctly entered. For a complete list of the hidden fields you can use and their syntax, contact your ISP. Some examples given here may need to be modified: for example, RECIPIENT may have to read REPLY TO or something similar, depending on the script your ISP uses.

The Hidden Field icon as placed in a form. All your hidden fields –like all your other form elements – will need to be contained within the red dotted box that shows the form in your page, although it is not important where a hidden field is placed in the form itself.

This column of boxes and buttons is not very attractive. You are unable to sort your form elements easily.

HOW MANY AND WHERE?

You can place as many hidden fields in your form as you want. Be careful, though – in the case of the NOBLANK parameter for instance – and make sure that you type the name of the text box correctly. If you do not, the web browser will complain and you will get an error message saying that the form couldn't be processed.

DESIGNING A FORM

If you followed the examples in this book and created a form by adding elements one after the other, you should get a page that looks something like this:

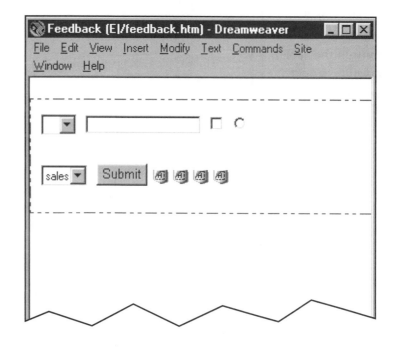

SEE WHAT IS HIDDEN

If you cannot see a hidden field in your page, it is because the View Invisible Elements option is off. Turn it on either by typing Shift+Ctrl+I or selecting VIEW/INVISIBLE ELEMENTS from the main menu bar.

To avoid the problem of having a jumbled-up form, put all the elements in a table and put the table into the form. With a bit of practice you will be able to design a decent form. Place each form element in an individual table cell, which can have all normal cell attributes (colour, indenting etc.). Because you will be using a table, you will be able to add pictures and text to your form and make it consistent instead of a collection of disjointed components.

1 Put all your form elements in a table, tidy things up and place your table in the form. The various elements in the table still have their own attributes and functionality.

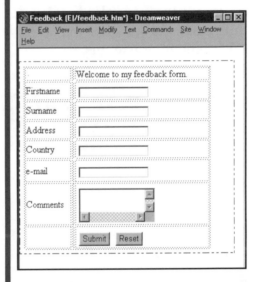

2 Liven up your table with graphics and other elements. A Help button has been added that will open a help page in a new window.

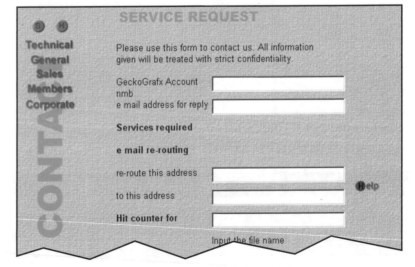

Your buttons, properly labelled, can act as hyperlink triggers.

ATTACHING ACTIONS TO A FORM ELEMENT

Form elements can be used outside forms when the information input by your visitor doesn't need to be processed by a CGI script. Sometimes, a button or a list will look better and more efficient than an image: for a hyperlink for instance. If this is the case in your site, you can place an element in a layer wherever you need in the page and attach a behaviour to it, in the same way you can attach a behaviour (or action) to any component of your site. You won't need to add a form to your page and are not restricted to placing the element inside that dotted line.

To do this, first place your form element in a layer and place the layer where it is supposed to go in your page. Remember that the label that goes in it will be displayed with a special font. Then go to the Behaviors tab (F8) and select an action from the list by clicking on the ± sign, for example Go to URL (which is in fact a straight hyperlink, as it will tell the button to display a given HTML file). One thing you won't have much control over, contrary to a mouse event for instance, is the type of behaviour – the Event – this Action can be triggered by. Although you can use a behaviour other than onClick to trigger the action, it is not really recommended.

The types of behaviours that can be attached to a button are limited. It is best to stick to onClick, for ease of use.

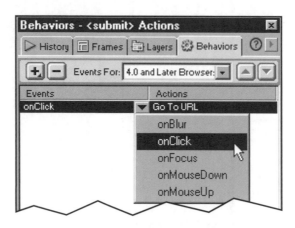

JAVA, JAVA SCRIPT AND ACTIONS

Dreamweaver 3 and other web design programs will pepper your site with JAVAScript. Things such as forms, buttons and rollovers are not made with HTML code but JAVAScript and are seamlessly integrated into your pages.

JAVA is a very powerful yet relatively simple programming language developed by Sun Microsystems. With it, you can create applets (small programs), to use on the web. JAVA applets do not appear in your pages themselves: they are called up, just like a CGI script. If you have been browsing the Web, you may have come across a site that offers you the chance to play with a Rubik's Cube. This is done using JAVA, and so are the help files in Dreamweaver 3.

Site Management

🖭 Applet started

Every time you see this at the bottom of your web browser's window, you'll know you are dealing with JAVA.

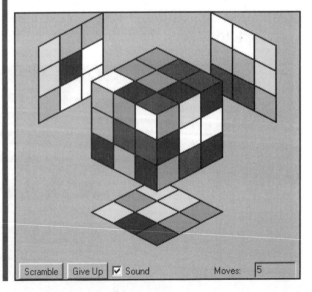

Scramble | Give Up | ☑ Sound | Moves: | 5

An example of a JAVA application. You can play with a Rubik's Cube to your heart's content over the web.

JAVASCRIPT

JAVAScript is an altogether different kettle of beans (JAVA applets are commonly called "beans"). JAVAScript appears in the coding of your pages themselves and will perform various commands for you without having to pass through an external program, script or applet. If you have been following the instructions in this book, you have used JAVAScript already.

An example of what a JAVAScript looks like, taken from a page created with Dreamweaver 3.

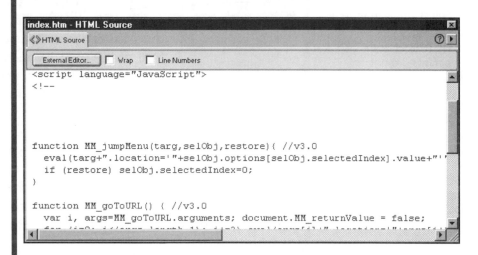

JAVAScript is recognized by all recent web browsers and will greatly enhance the look and feel of your site. There are a lot of free JAVAScript codes on the web, with precise and easy step-by-step descriptions of how to set them up in your pages. They will put a clock on your page, provide you with a timer to redirect your visitor to a new page, let you determine what to do if your visitor is using a Windows machine or a Macintosh… in short, a script can add even more to your site.

A WORLD OF ACTIONS

You do not need to learn programming to use JAVAScript. Dreamweaver 3 will do it for you. An example of embedding JAVAScript in your page is when you use actions. Swapping one image for another depending on the position of the mouse is an Action, and it uses JAVAScript. It is now time to learn a bit more about the <u>Behaviors</u> tab that we keep using.

The <u>Behaviors</u> palette, from where you assign actions to objects. Summon this by choosing <u>WINDOW/BEHAVIORS</u> from the main menu bar. Click on the ± sign to get a list of actions. Select the web browser you need and remember: some actions are not supported by all web browsers.

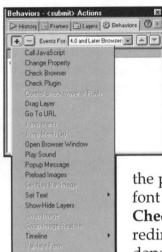

Here is a list of the actions from the tab that you are likely to use:

Call JavaScript: if you have imported a JAVAScript into your page, you can assign this action to an image or a button, for instance: when the button is clicked on, the JAVAScript starts.

Change property: this will change the properties such as the height, width or font of the object you specify.

Check browser: this powerful action will redirect your visitor to different pages depending on which web browser they use. This is useful because not all web browsers behave in the same way.

Check Plugin: a plugin is an external program that some web pages require to display correctly. Check if a plugin exists on your visitor's machine and if it does, automatically redirect your visitor to the page containing the component that requires it.

Control Shockwave or Flash: if you have inserted a Shockwave or Flash object in your page, you can control their behaviour via a button.

Go to URL: You have used this action already. This will act as a hyperlink for a button or web element.

Jump Menu: this will create a list of hyperlinks.

Open Browser Window: use this action to open your HTML pages in a brand new window and to control its parameters.

Play Sound: play a sound.

Popup Message: have a window pop up with some extra information in it.

Show-Hide Layers: the layers you have inserted in your pages might not need to be visible all the time. Switch them on or off according to your needs.

Swap Image: this action is used to create rollovers.

Timeline: make a Timeline animation jump to a particular frame or start and stop it.

Each action listed has a specific argument and parameter to enter. It is advisable that you start your site the easy way and build up confidence, then start adding some of the more complex actions to it. Although most of these actions are quite self-explanatory in their implementation, at some point a basic knowledge of HTML may be required for some of them.

To successfully set up an action, you have to answer these three questions:

What will be the object that will call the Action (an image, some text, a button?)

What will the Action be?

What Event will trigger the Action?

EVENTS

You have already encountered a list of Events. An Event is what your visitor will have to do to perform an Action. It can be a click on an image, on a button, the resizing of the page etc. It can also be when the page is loaded or exited. The events are available from the <u>Behavior</u> tab. Dreamweaver 3 will assign an Event to your Action automatically and most of the time the default settings will be the ones you need. If you do need to change them, first select the Action by clicking on it in the <u>Behavior</u> tab and click the down arrow next to it.

1 View the actions available for a given object.

This is the Event part.

This is the action part.

Change the Event to the one you need by picking one from the list.

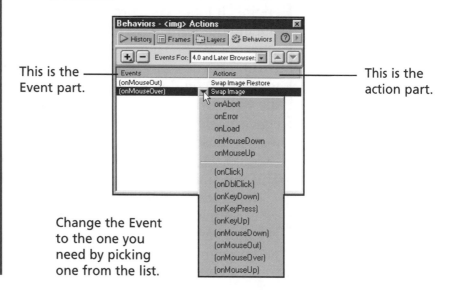

META TAGS

The last thing you need to do with your site is to add a few meta tags. These are special HTML tags that will contain and transfer some special information about your page to people searching for information over the Internet.

There are two types of simple meta tags you are likely to use in your site: description and keywords. They will help you publish your page to the web with a maximum of effect.

DESCRIPTION
The description of a page is the short few lines that appear underneath the URL when you look for a site in a search engine. It looks very professional to put a description of your site in your homepage (a homepage is usually a welcome page – the one your visitor will be taken to when they go to your URL). This description doesn't need to be very long, nor too technical. You don't want to explain your entire site, just entice the web surfer to have a look at what you have on offer. A concise, relevant paragraph is what you are aiming for. To insert a description in your page, select INSERT/HEAD/DESCRIPTION from the main menu bar. This will open the Insert Description dialog box.

The description will not appear in your page itself, but in your coding. If you want to see what it looks like, click on the HTML symbol on the Launcher palette. The HTML Source box will pop up. Insert your description as described and watch it being incorporated into your HTML code.

1 The <u>Insert</u> <u>Description</u> dialog box. Type in the description of your site in the <u>Description</u> box and press <u>OK</u>.

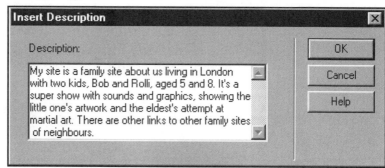

2 Click on the HTML symbol to bring up the HTML editor shown below.

3 See how your code is inserted into your HTML code as you type some text in the <u>Description</u> dialog box (shown above). This is where your description will be inserted: in the <u>HEAD</u> section of your code.

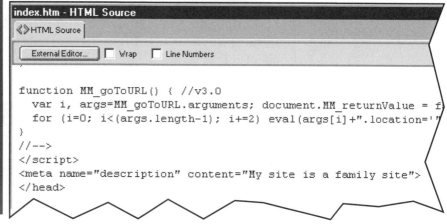

```
function MM_goToURL() { //v3.0
   var i, args=MM_goToURL.arguments; document.MM_returnValue = f
   for (i=0; i<(args.length-1); i+=2) eval(args[i]+".location='"
}
//-->
</script>
<meta name="description" content="My site is a family site">
</head>
```

You can leave the <u>HTML Source</u> window open and watch what happens to the HTML code when you add elements to your page. Each time you click on an element (a layer, an image, some text, a timeline, etc.), the relevant HTML tag will be highlighted in this window.

1 Clicking <u>INSERT/HEAD/ KEYWORDS</u> will bring up the <u>Insert Keywords</u> dialog box. Type your keywords in the text box.

ADDING KEYWORDS

Keywords are the words search engines will look for when performing a search. If your site has a keyword list that contains "Blue" and a web surfer performs a search for, say, "The deep blue sea", your site will be listed in their search results. To add keywords to your site, select <u>INSERT/HEAD/KEYWORDS</u> from the main menu bar.

You need type in your keywords only once in your index.html page (assuming that this is your main, or home, page). If you need more than one keyword, separate them with a comma and a space. Some web browsers will simply ignore all your keywords if there are too many of them. It is better to select a few well-chosen words than to fill up the entire box with keywords.

MAXIMIZE YOUR CHANCES

Some web browsers will bypass keywords if there are too many of them. They will rely on the description instead. A good idea is to try to repeat the keywords in the description so that you are sure your site gets the notice it deserves. Ten is a reasonable maximum number of keywords.

PUBLISHING YOUR SITE

6

You didn't build your site just to have it sitting on your hard drive – you need to make your site accessible to more people. You will want to publish it on the Internet, the place where it belongs. Internet Service Providers provide you with web space, which is an amount of hard disk space on one of their computers. This is where your site is going to end up and everybody – no matter where they live or what time of day it is when they browse the web – will be able to access it.

ISPs AND ACCOUNTS

An ISP is an Internet Service Provider. They are the people who will provide a line from your computer to the rest of the world. You cannot do without registering with an ISP if you want to publish your site on the net, or even if you want to check it online.

There are basically two types of ISP: the ones you have to pay for the and ones you don't. Depending on your needs, you may feel you have to pay for your ISP. The main difference between the two types of ISP (apart from the price!) is that paying ISPs are generally easier (and usually cheaper) to contact in case of problems and are (probably) more dedicated to satisfying their customers. You are also less likely to have difficulty getting online with a paying ISP.

Free ISPs are flourishing. You have probably received a promotional CD from one company or another through the post, or been to a shop offering you free web access and free web space.

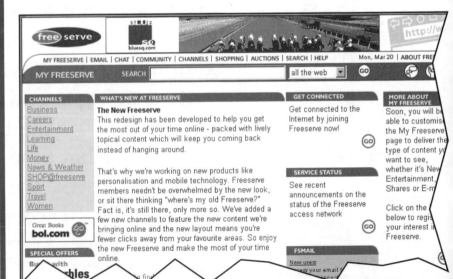

ACCOUNTS

Whether you choose to go for a free ISP or a paying one, you will have to sign up for an account with them. CDs that you get in the post, the ones found on magazines' covers or ones that you find in shops will contain all the information you need for doing this.

DOMAIN NAMES

If you do not have your own domain name, you will be assigned your ISP's andyour web address could look something like this: http://www.freeisp.com/users/myuserpage/index.html. This is quite an address to remember and there is no way you could have that printed on a business card. If you intend to build a professional or commercial site, you will have to get a domain name for it. A domain name is an account with a particular company that deals with domain registration. You choose a name for your domain (it will be translated into "www.yourdomain.com"), register it with any company that deals with this kind of operation for a fee, and each time somebody types this address, they will be redirected to your web pages stored on your ISP's web server. There will also be, in most cases, a fee to pay to your ISP to have them set up your domain name. These fees can be hefty, so shop around and think about whether you do need a domain name or not before committing yourself.

There are plenty of companies from which you can register domain names. The competition is fierce, so do shop around.

FTP

WWW, FTP, ISP, http. There are so many acronyms associated with the web that it is surprising that anyone involved with it can actually talk. Don't worry, though; everything is quite straightforward when it is time to put your site on the Internet, and most programs are easy to get hold of and easy to use. We'll start this section by explaining some of the terms that you'll need to be familiar with.

All connections to a web site through a web browser will use HTTP.

In order to communicate with one another, computers need a common language – a protocol – for their information to be written in. Your web browser deals mostly with one type of protocol, the HyperText Transfer Protocol, or HTTP. If you type an address in your browser such as www.companysoandso.com, it will automatically be translated into http://www.companysoandso.com. The prefix HTTP tells your browser that the files it is receiving are web pages for it to display – it is in HyperText Transfer Protocol mode. The hypertext language files transferred (HTML files) are opened and the information they contain are processed by the browser and displayed as web pages.

Typing "ftp" instead of "http://" in your browser's location field will instruct it to stop opening the files that it encounters. The browser is in FTP mode. Beware, though, that very few sites will give you free access to their files directly. You will normally need a password and a login name to download files.

This is an ftp site viewed from a web browser. The web pages (HTML files) are not opened and are seen as plain files instead.

FTP

FTP stands for File Transfer Protocol. It is a way for computers to transfer files to each other as opposed to displaying them on the screen as with HTTP. When in this mode, your browser knows that the files it receives are not to be displayed but saved on to your hard disk. An FTP address is different from a web address: the HTTP part, no longer useful, is replaced by FTP. The FTP site of companysoandso would be ftp.companysoandso.com.

WEB SITES AND FTP SITES

A web site is what you are building with the help of this book. It is the collection of files in various formats (HTML, image files, archives, sounds, etc.). When you sign up with an ISP, you get some free web space. This web space is your FTP site. It is a portion of your ISP's computer's hard disk space reserved solely for your use.

AN FTP SITE, WHY?

Your web site cannot be accessed by anyone but you until it is published on the web. When you surf the web, you connect to computers (servers) across the world. It is on these servers' hard disks that web sites are stored. These servers are connected 24 hours a day, so anyone can access the files stored there at any time. "Publishing" your site means to transfer it (upload it) to one of these hard disks; in other words, the FTP site your Internet Service Provider has given you.

INTRODUCTION TO NETWORKING

As you learned in Chapter 1, the world wide web is a huge network of computers linked together. When you surf the web, you network your local computer via your phone line to your ISP, which in turn links you to the other networked remote computers around the world.

Your computer is said to be "local" because you sit in front of it and you work on it. A remote computer is the computer you are connected to over a network. Depending on the privileges – the level of control – you have on a server, you can perform file operations (copying, deleting, renaming, etc.) or even run programs that are installed on the remote computer.

SERVER AND CLIENT

You wouldn't be far from the truth if you were to compare these two terms to what happens in a restaurant: you are the client and the waiter serves your food. In computer terms, it means that you – the client – connect to a remote server that is going to deliver files to your local computer. File operations from a client to a server are limited to getting files. If you have an account with the server, your login and password will let you have access to the server's hard disks to copy your files there. Your ISP is a server and delivers all the web pages that it is storing to whoever requests them. It is a one-way connection, though: you connect to your ISP and browse their hard disk for the web pages that are stored there, or you copy your own files on to them via FTP, but there is no way that your ISP is going to come and check what you have on yours.

WHY DO I NEED A SERVER?

Below is a diagram that shows pretty much what happens when you surf the Internet:

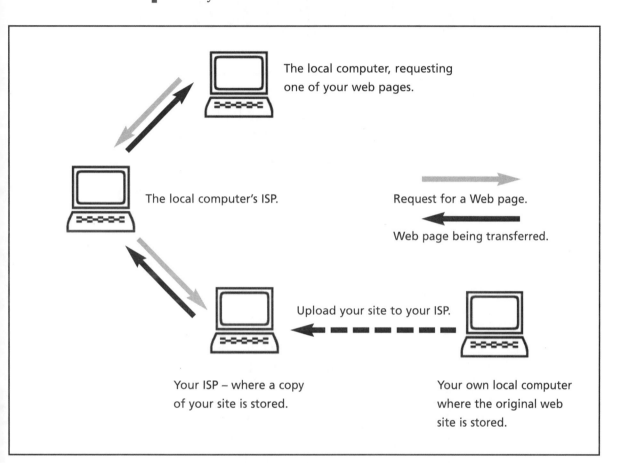

The local computer, requesting one of your web pages.

The local computer's ISP.

Request for a Web page.

Web page being transferred.

Upload your site to your ISP.

Your ISP – where a copy of your site is stored.

Your own local computer where the original web site is stored.

A computer's request for your web site is relayed by servers all over the world until it reaches its destination: the web space that your ISP provides you with and on which you have copied your site.

As you can see, everybody can connect to your ISP via the web. You upload your site via FTP to your personal web space and your ISP will make it available to the rest of the world. If you do not, people will not be able to access the files because you will not be connected to the web. And even if you do connect to the web from time to time, your computer is not set up with the necessary protocols that would enable others to connect to it. Think of your ISP as a repository – an interactive gallery where everybody can admire your creation.

FTP SOFTWARE

To upload files to your FTP site you need a special program called an FTP program, or at least a program with a special feature capable of handling file transfer operations. There are plenty of such easy-to-use programs available to you, such as CuteFTP for Windows and Fetch for Macintosh. Some web design programs are so clever that they let you build your site and upload it too.

Most examples in this book will come from Dreamweaver and CuteFTP, distributed by GlobalSCAPE, which is one of the most widely-used FTP packages available for Windows. It is shareware, which means that you can try it for a while and then you have to buy it if you want to carry on using it. It is quite cheap and user-friendly. You do not have to get this particular program, though. Browse the web for another one, check your favourite computer magazine's cover CDs, or rely on Dreamweaver 3's FTP facilities if you want.

CONNECTING TO YOUR FTP SITE

You connect to your FTP site the same way you connect to the web in general – by using your phone line. You will have to

One of the easiest and most complete FTP packages on the market for Windows-based machines: CuteFTP.

enter your ISP's computer network to copy files to their hard drives, so before you start anything you will need their authorization. You will also need to know where your personal web space actually is. So ask your ISP for a login and a password. They will give you an address, a login and a password that will be yours and yours alone. Don't let anyone else have access to this information – you never know what may become of your site if you share your logon and password details. Once your site is on your ISP's hard disk, it is just as safe as if it was still sitting in your own computer: nobody but you will be able to access your FTP site and modify anything you have put there.

WHAT CAN YOU DO WITH YOUR FTP SITE?

Once you are connected to your FTP site, you will be able to use the hard disk space that the ISP has reserved for you in the same way you use your hard disk on your own computer. You will be able to copy and delete files and folders as well as creating folders.

STRUCTURE OF AN FTP PACKAGE

Whatever your FTP package is, it will most likely be split into two main windows: one for the remote site and one for the local site. The local site is the one you are working with, the one on your computer's hard drive. The remote one (when you are publishing a site) is the one that lives on your ISP's hard drive. Your task when publishing your site will be to transfer it from the local to the remote system. You don't have to do anything fancy; just copy the files across as they are.

DOWNLOAD AND UPLOAD

These are two terms you need to understand in order to become proficient in web publishing. Downloading means getting files from another computer to yours. You view files when you browse the web and you download files when you take them from one computer or a server and put them on to yours. Uploading means putting files from your computer on to someone else's. You do this to place your site on your ISP's hard disk so that these files become available to anyone connected to the Internet.

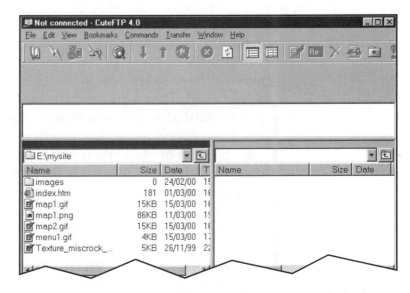

The main FTP window in CuteFTP (above) and Dreamweaver (below).
It is called the <u>Site Files</u> window in Dreamweaver.
When uploaded, the files used in your site will appear in the right-hand
window of CuteFTP, and the left-hand window of Dreamweaver.

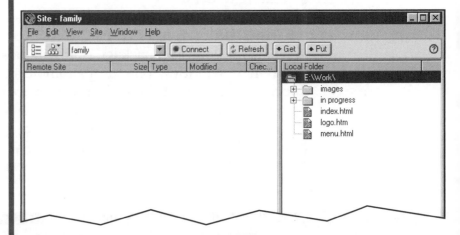

SETTING UP YOUR FTP PROGRAM

Whatever the FTP program you use, there is some essential
information for uploading your site successfully. The
information you need to have is your login (sometimes called
your username or user ID), your password, the URL of your
FTP site and the location of your root directory.

The first time you run CuteFTP, the <u>Connection Wizard</u> will pop up and ask you a few questions so that it can set up your connection to your ISP and place it in a bookmark. When you have done this for a particular server, instead of retyping the information each time you use CuteFTP you will be taken straight to the FTP site of your choice when you connect.

1 CuteFTP's <u>Connection Wizard</u> will help you set up your FTP options. Once the information required by the <u>Connection Wizard</u> has been entered, click on <u>Next</u> to go to the next screen.

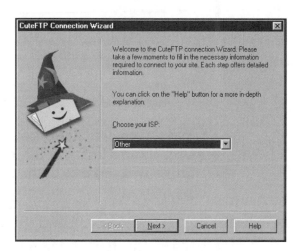

After entering a useful name for your connection on screen 2, you will be asked for the URL of your FTP site, which you should have received from your ISP.

2 Enter your FTP address, which should look like your web address except that it will probably have "ftp" instead of the "www" at the beginning.

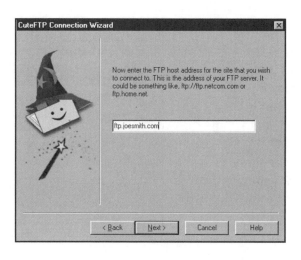

3 The next step is to type your login and password (CuteFTP uses the term User ID for your login). You have to type your User ID and your password exactly as they were given you by your ISP.

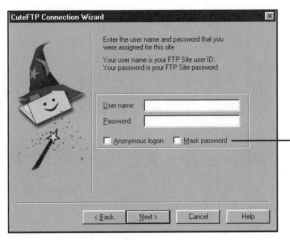

If you check this box, you will see a series of asterisks instead of a series of letters and numbers in the Password field.

Some servers will allow you to log on to their network without a User ID and login. In this case, most of the time your email address will serve as both. These servers are usually set up by big organizations such as NASA for instance, where you can go and download pictures, or by computer software and hardware companies from which you can get updates for your system. This type of login is called an anonymous login and you should check the Anonymous box if you want to link to one of them. An anonymous login does not let you perform any file transfer operation other than downloading. As you are going to upload your site to your FTP site, leave this button unchecked.

4 Screen 3. The default local directory is your root folder; that is, the folder on your hard disk that contains all the files you need for your web site.

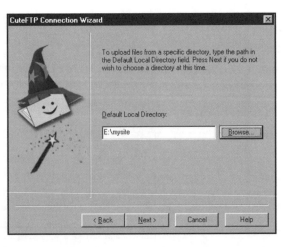

Type the path of the root directory in the box or browse your hard disk.

One more screen and you are done. Now that the information is entered, CuteFTP will give you two more options. One is the option to connect to your FTP site as soon as you run CuteFTP. If you select this option, you will have to be connected to the web beforehand. The other option is to add an entry in the context menu, the one that pops up when you right-click on a file.

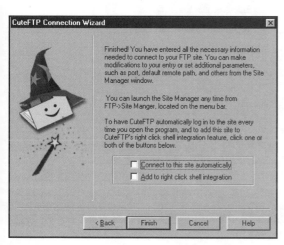

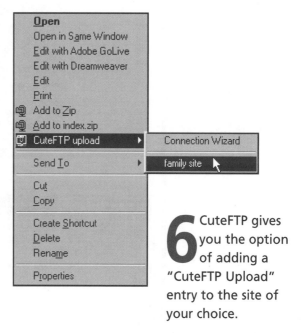

5 Select the way CuteFTP will behave when you run it.

6 CuteFTP gives you the option of adding a "CuteFTP Upload" entry to the site of your choice.

If you wish to use Dreamweaver to upload your site, you can. The information described in the previous pages will have to be entered in the Define Sites dialog box, accessible by clicking on SITE/DEFINE SITES from the main menu bar. First select the site you want to use and click on Edit. You will get the Site Definition dialog box for the site you selected. Go to the left-hand box – the Category box – and click on Web Server Info as shown in the next illustration. Type the same information you used in the CuteFTP section above in the relevant text fields and click on OK.

Once everything is set up the way you want it to be, go back to the Site Files dialog box, click on the Connect button and start uploading your files. You will have to be already connected to the Internet before attempting an FTP connection through Dreamweaver.

1 In the Site Definition dialog box type your login, password and your FTP site address. Leave the other boxes to their default values. When you are done, click on OK and then on Done in the box that follows.

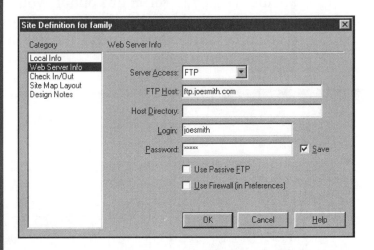

2 In the Site window, click on Connect to get on to your FTP server. Then just copy across the files for your site.

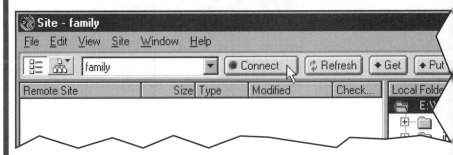

UPLOADING FROM WEB PAGES
Some free ISPs will not let you use an FTP program to upload your files to your FTP site. They will provide you with a special web page to which you can log in and do it from your web browser. This page is likely to be called the "Site Manager" page or something similar. This process is often limited in the sense that you can rarely create your own directories within such sites and that is a hindrance, especially if your site has been devised with folders. Before you sign up with an ISP, even a free one, check that you can use all the features of an FTP program. OSPs such as AOL will also present you with a special feature to transfer your files.

PATHS

7

The web can seem like a maze where hundreds of sites appear when you only searched for one. Perform a search for a particular topic and page after page of links appear in your browser. So how do they do that? How can you click on a link and amid the millions of pages available, get exactly the page you are looking for? To understand this, you will have to learn acronyms such as URL and IP and the way files are stored on the web. More importantly, you will learn why you can't get lost.

PATHS
AND URLs

You have already encountered these terms in this book and now is the time to shed some light on this strange URL thing, because understanding URLs and paths is the key to navigating the web successfully.

Navigating the web is a matter of finding some files stored somewhere across the world. You follow the same process when you open files on your local computer. You use a path to tell it the file you want is on hard disk so-and-so, in such-and-such folder, itself perhaps inside another folder, and so forth.

PATHS
When running Windows 98 and double-clicking on <u>My Computer</u>, you get a list of all the storage media available on your computer. These are usually your floppy disk, your main hard disk from which Windows runs, your CD or DVD ROMs and a few special Windows folders. At the top of this window is the <u>Address Bar</u>, as shown below.

If you cannot see the Address Bar, go to the main menu bar and select VIEW/TOOLBARS/ ADDRESS BAR.

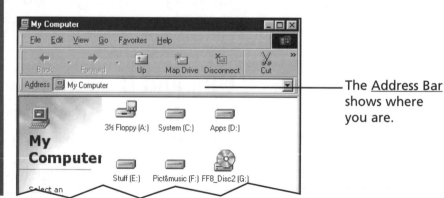

The <u>Address Bar</u> shows where you are.

This <u>Address Bar</u> will show the current directory (the current folder) you are working with. If you double-click on the hard drive "C", this <u>Address Bar</u> will display "C:\". Notice how this looks like the "http://" you get in a web address.

This is the root directory of drive C. The root directory is the part of the hard disk where all the other folders in this hard disk will be contained.

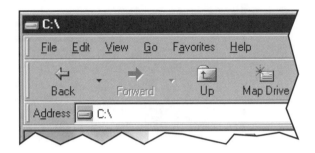

Now double-click on a folder in this window. This will open the folder and the <u>Address Bar</u> will reflect this change by displaying the new directory.

In this illustration, you are now in "C:\my directory\".

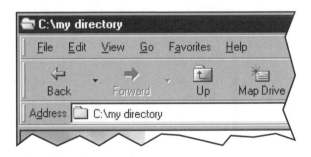

The path for a file situated in this folder will be "C:\my directory\" followed by the name of the file (i.e. "C:\my directory\my file.txt").

WHERE IS B?

Your floppy disk will always be labelled "A" and your first hard disk "C". So where is "B"? No, computer manufacturers don't have anything against Bs. When the first computers were built, they were not very powerful and didn't have any hard disk, just a floppy drive. In order to copy a floppy disk, you had to copy its contents into the computer memory, swap this floppy disk for a blank one and copy the files across. The computer would name the first floppy disk A and the second B, although there was only one drive, A. Since then things have improved a lot, but the naming convention has remained.

URL

URL stands for Uniform Resource Locator. It is more commonly called an address, or a web address. As for a normal computer, it is a path to a particular file. A URL is made of a minimum of four parts, as shown below:

Here is a URL in a Microsoft IE 5 Address Bar.

The first part is the Protocol name, usually http:.

The "www" part tells your browser where the site is located: in this case the World Wide Web.

"geckografx" is the host name – the name of the organization that stores your site (usually the ISP).

".com" specifies the type of organization this site belongs to. In this case, it is a commercial site.

You can see that this address looks like a path for a file on your computer, which in a way it is. The name of your site's files and folders will follow an address such as the one shown above. This is the reason why you sometimes get very long addresses in the location bar of your web browser when you surf the web: free ISPs have a lot of clients and each client is reserved a portion of their many hard disks. These hard disks are themselves divided into smaller portions. Your site hosted by a free ISP could give you a web address looking, for instance, like "http://www.freeisp.com/computer12/harddisk20/partition12/usersmith/index.html"… although it wouldn't look very impressive.

DO WITHOUT "http://"   _ 🗗 ☒

In a new browser window, you don't need to type "http://" before your address. www.mycompany.com will suffice. The browser will understand that it has to go in "http mode".

IP ADDRESSES

One last term you might come across while using FTP or web design programs (and web browsers), is IP address. An IP address is a number assigned to each and every computer connected to a network, be it the web, an intranet, a Local Area Network (LAN) or a simple one to one connection between only two systems. This number is unique to each

Check your current IP address via an MS DOS prompt. The fourth row of numbers is your IP address (in this case, 212.49.233.146).

```
MS-DOS Prompt
Auto

Microsoft(R) Windows 98
    (C)Copyright Microsoft Corp 1981-1999.

C:\WINDOWS>route print

Active Routes:

  Network Address          Netmask  Gateway Address        Interface  Metric
        0.0.0.0          0.0.0.0   212.49.233.146   212.49.233.146       1
      127.0.0.0        255.0.0.0        127.0.0.1        127.0.0.1       1
   212.49.233.0    255.255.255.0   212.49.233.146   212.49.233.146       1
 212.49.233.146  255.255.255.255        127.0.0.1        127.0.0.1       1
 212.49.233.255  255.255.255.255   212.49.233.146   212.49.233.146       1
      224.0.0.0        224.0.0.0   212.49.233.146   212.49.233.146       1
255.255.255.255  255.255.255.255   212.49.233.146   212.49.233.146       1

C:\WINDOWS>
```

computer and made of four sets of three digits ranging from 0 to 255 (for example 120.0.155.222). Your computer, when you connect to the web, has an IP address too. Your ISP assigns it to you automatically. To see what your IP address is, connect to the web and press your Start button on Windows Taskbar. Select PROGRAMS/MS DOS PROMPT. In the black DOS window, type route print. A set of numbers will appear.

Connecting to site 216.15.185.97

You can see the IP address of a site as you connect to it by looking at the bottom of your browser window.

At the bottom of your web browser, when you request a connection to a site, you will see the IP address of the site in the bottom bar. Because web addresses are easier to remember and because they are more aesthetic, IP addresses are translated by the domain name companies from numbers to words and vice versa.

USING YOUR SERVER

The web space on your server will behave just like your hard disk. You will need to duplicate your hard disk exactly on to your server. If you placed images and sounds into folders on your hard disk, these folders will have to be created on your server.

You do not have to create your root folder on your server. If your site is contained in a folder called "My site", you do not need to create a "My site" folder on your server.

1 Tell CuteFTP where your files are.

EDIT YOUR SITE

We looked at CuteFTP in Chapter 6. We will now use this to upload a site. Connect to the Internet with CuteFTP. Now that you have created a connection, you need to arrange your CuteFTP windows and tell it where your local site is. In the Site Settings dialog box (which you will get automatically when you start CuteFTP), click on your site and then on the EDIT button. As you have already entered the required information to connect to your FTP site in the previous section, you are ready to start your uploading section. So press on Connect and watch the top window.

2 In the <u>Settings</u> dialog box, type the path to your root folder in the <u>Default Local Directory</u> field (or browse your hard disk) and press <u>OK</u>.

3 Messages informing you of the various steps in the transferring of your files will appear in the top window.

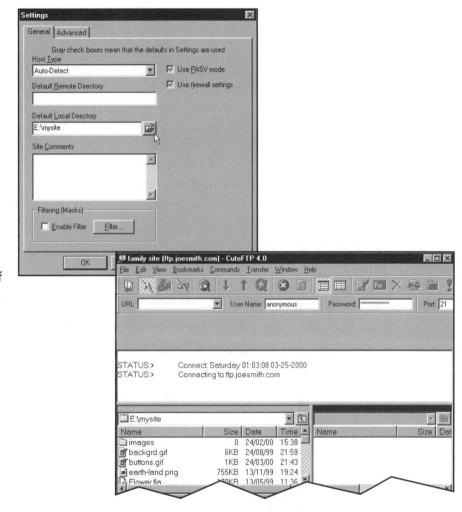

4 Once your connection has been accepted, you will get a "terminal window" that will show various pieces of information about your web server, such as the type of server, the date and other things.

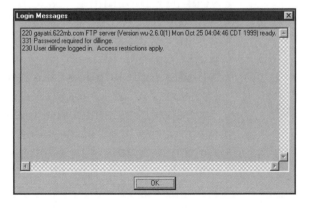

Depending on the size of your screen, you might have to select <u>WINDOWS/TOGGLE LOCAL</u> from the main menu bar (or press <u>F6</u>). This will split the middle window in two: the left side for the local directory and the right side for the remote directory. Drag on the centre border of the middle window to move it left and right, thus enlarging or shrinking the windows (in fact, you can do this with all the windows' borders in CuteFTP). The right window that was empty now contains the list of the files and directory present on the remote computer.

You have now four windows, each of them displaying different information.

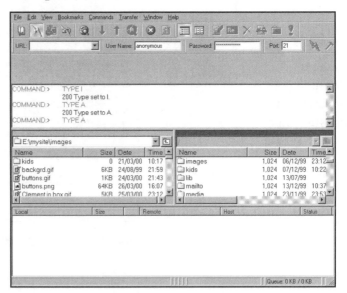

Top window: this window will display the various commands your FTP program gives to the server.

Middle left window: the local directory. Use the icon showing a folder with an arrow in it to move one level up in your directory structure.

Middle right window: the remote directory. If you keep pressing on the <u>Level up</u> icon, there will come a point when access will be denied because you are trying to get out of the web space your ISP has allotted to you.

Bottom window: this window will show you all the transfers actually active or queued (a transfer is queued when it has to wait for a previous transfer to finish).

CREATING REMOTE FOLDERS

By clicking inside a window you choose to work on your remote or local site. Choose to work on the remote site. At the top of these windows sits the main toolbar, from which you are going to select the Make new directory icon as shown below. This will bring up the Create new directory dialog box (a directory is another name for a folder).

Duplicating your root folder is the key to publishing your site successfully. If your pages work on your system and you upload them in the exact folders on your server, they will work there too. As soon as a new folder is created, it will appear in the list. They can be opened by double-clicking on them the same way you would with a folder on your hard disk. If you make a mistake, right-click on the folder and select Delete from the context menu (most of the file operation options are accessible through this menu). You can also highlight it and press the Delete key.

1 Click on the Make new directory icon.

2 Type the name of your new directory.

UPLOADING YOUR PAGES

Now that your workplace has been duplicated from your local computer to the remote one, all you have to do is to transfer the files across. This is the last step before having your site available on the web.

There are a few techniques you can use to do this. The easiest way is to simply drag and drop the files from one window (the local site window) to the other (the remote site window). You can drag a file on to a folder and it will be moved inside it. If you do this, the destination folder will be highlighted and a small ± icon will appear alongside your mouse pointer.

Another technique is to double-click on a file. It will automatically be transferred to the current directory. You can upload whole folders this way too: first CuteFTP will create the new folder and then upload the files into it.

MULTIPLE TRANSFERS

Transfering one file at a time would be very tedious and time consuming. You can select multiple files from either window by Ctrl-clicking on them, or you can click on a file and then Shift-click on another and all the files in between will be selected. Take the whole lot and drag them across to the remote window. In the bottom window, all the files you have selected for upload will be listed as queuing.

CUTE FTP PROMPTS

Every time you perform a copy operation, CuteFTP will prompt you for a confirmation. This can be irritating after a while and you can change this from the Settings dialog box, under Prompts.

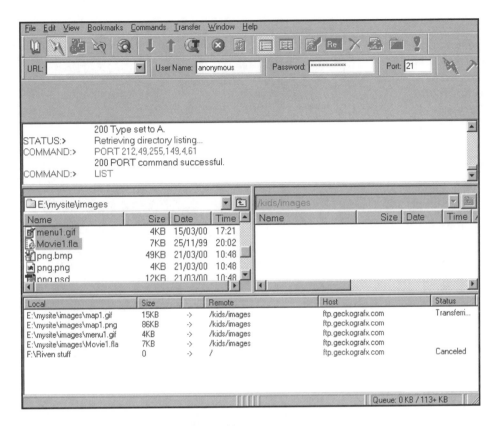

File   Edit   View   Bookmarks   Commands   Transfer   Window   Help

URL: User Name: anonymous   Password: ××××××××××××   Port: 21

STATUS:>   200 Type set to A.
          Retrieving directory listing...
COMMAND:> PORT 212,49,255,149,4,61
          200 PORT command successful.
COMMAND:> LIST

E:\mysite\images   /kids/images

Name	Size	Date	Time	Name	Size	Date	Time
menu1.gif	4KB	15/03/00	17:21				
Movie1.fla	7KB	25/11/99	20:02				
png.bmp	49KB	21/03/00	10:48				
png.png	4KB	21/03/00	10:48				
png.psd	12KB	21/03/00	10:48				

Local	Size		Remote	Host	Status
E:\mysite\images\map1.gif	15KB	->	/kids/images	ftp.geckografx.com	Transferri...
E:\mysite\images\map1.png	86KB	->	/kids/images	ftp.geckografx.com	
E:\mysite\images\menu1.gif	4KB	->	/kids/images	ftp.geckografx.com	
E:\mysite\images\Movie1.fla	7KB	->	/kids/images	ftp.geckografx.com	
F:\Riven stuff	0	->	/	ftp.geckografx.com	Canceled

Queue: 0 KB / 113+ KB

Uploading using CuteFTP. Each file will wait for the previous one to finish transferring before starting.

USING DREAMWEAVER

The same process applies to uploading pages using any FTP package. The windows and buttons may look different and have different names, but the basic idea is always the same. You can use Dreamweaver to transfer the files too. This is done through the Site Files tab, called up by pressing F5 or selecting WINDOW/SITE FILES from the main menu bar. If you entered the details for your site when you followed the steps earlier, all you will have to do now is to click on the Connect button.

FTP OVER EMAIL   _ ☐ ×

Email servers do not accept big messages. If you have a file to transfer to a friend that will not fit in an email, put it on your FTP site (compress it first – with WinZip for instance – so it's not too big) and give them the URL of the file. They will be able to download it from their web browser.

In Dreamweaver, once
the site information is
entered, click on
<u>Connect</u> to hook up to
your web server.

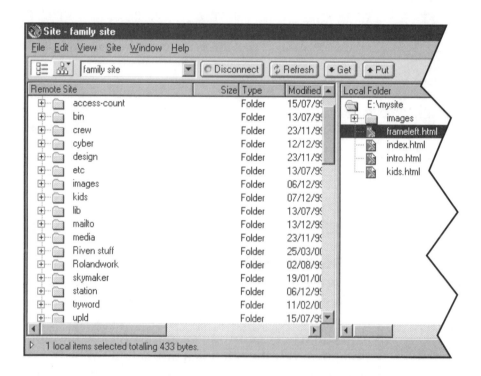

As for CuteFTP, the
remote site and the
local site will be
displayed in separate
windows. In
Dreamweaver, the
layout adopted is
that of the standard
Windows Explorer.

Click on the <u>+</u> and <u>-</u> symbols to expand or collapse the folders.
Once again you will have to drag the files across from one
window to another.

Once your site is uploaded, you can now check it with
<u>Check Links Sitewide</u> to make sure you haven't forgotten any
files on the way. Select <u>SITE/CHECK LINKS SITEWIDE</u> from
the main menu bar or press <u>Ctrl+F8</u>. A window will appear
with a summary of all the mistakes, if any, the check has
found in your uploaded site.

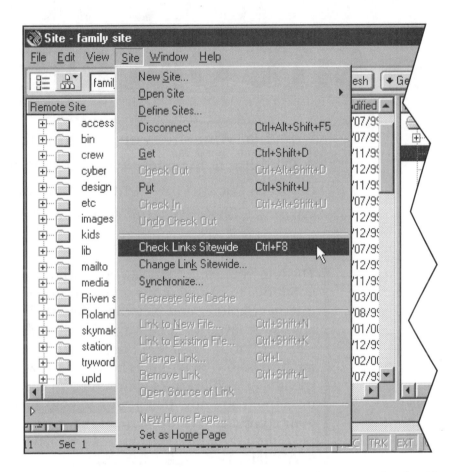

Check that everything is present and where it is supposed to be. If an error is listed, you'll need to find a missing picture or page and put it in the place that Dreamweaver expects to find it.

DOWNLOADING FILES

To download a file, simply drag from the remote site to the local site window in any FTP program. All the operations possible from local to remote are available the other way around. You can use this feature to download files that a colleague has put in the FTP site for you, or download a particular file if you lost it or modified it without having done a backup first.

CHECKING YOUR SITE ONLINE

Now that your site is up, it is time to check that everything is in order. You can send a form and see if it comes back to the right recipient and check the various CGI scripts and JAVA applets you might have inserted in your site.

The tool you use for this is your faithful web browser. It is a good idea to run your site online through both Microsoft Internet Explorer and Netscape, though, because they do not always behave the same way. The other thing you will need is a text editor or a pen and paper to jot down all the things that might possibly be wrong. The very best would be to go to a friend's or a colleague's computer and check your site on their machine. You know that your site works and looks good on your computer, but what about theirs?

STARTING THE WEB BROWSER
If you are not one hundred per cent familiar with the use of a web browser, now is the time to spend some time on it. Double-click on the browser's icon on your desktop and get things running. Once the start page is loaded, go to the Address Bar and select the current address by double-clicking on it. Type the URL of your site over it.

1 Start by typing the URL of your site in the Address Bar.

As soon as the URL is entered, press <u>Return</u> on your keyboard and watch your site load. The checking process will start right there, before any image appears on the page. What you will get will be a series of boxes where the images will be when they have finished downloading. You have the opportunity to see whether the alternate text you have set up while your images load is correct and relevant.

2 Check that the alternative text you have set for your images is accurate.

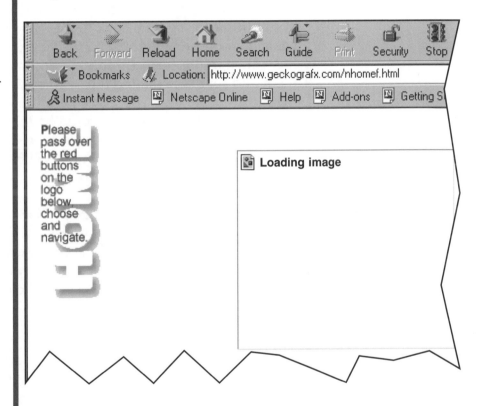

3 The <u>Refresh</u> and <u>Reload</u> button will become very handy later on when you modify your pages.

One by one the images will appear, along with the text and the background image. Take a good look. Is everything where it is supposed to be? Are there any images you can't see? Is the frameset correctly set up? Are the scrollbars present? Now resize the window. If you are using Netscape, you might need to hit the <u>Refresh</u> button after resizing. This operation is not necessary with Internet Explorer. This will tell you whether your tables, if you have any, are properly indented.

HYPERLINKS

Repeat this process for all the pages you have created. This will also check the working of your hyperlinks. If you get the infamous "Error 404" page, you will need to work on the faulty (broken) link. Remember that what you see is what millions of other people will get: if you cannot access a page because a link doesn't work, they won't either, no matter what machine or what browser they use. So click on ALL the links, even if it means coming back to the same page over and over again. Check the hyperlinks in the frames to see if the relevant links open in the correct frames. If you have mailtos, click on them and send an email to the recipient, even if it is just to say "This a web site test. You do not need to reply to this message" kind of thing. You could have typed the email address wrongly and this is not the sort of thing that Dreamweaver's built-in dictionary will have picked out when you did a spell check on your page.

4 Use the <u>Back</u> button to navigate your site more easily. If you have a hyperlink in every page that always goes to the same page (the home page for instance), using the <u>Back</u> button will be faster than repeating the same sequence of clicks that got you there in the first place.

5 Check for any of these, the missing image symbol – in IE on the left, or in Netscape on the right.

MISSING IMAGES

If, while you navigate your site, you come across an empty image box with a red cross in it or a broken image, that means you have a missing image.

The presence of the missing image symbol can be due to a few things. More than likely you forgot to upload the image file or it has been uploaded in the wrong folder. Go back to your FTP program, upload the missing image and click on the Refresh button on your browser's toolbar.

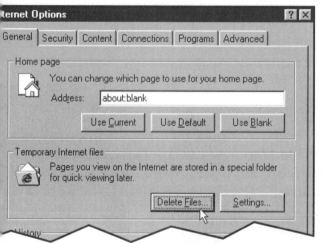

YOUR BROWSER'S CACHE

If you have modified an image after checking your site and still can't see the modified version but only the old one even, when you refresh your page, you will have to clear the browser's cache. The cache is a special folder on your computer where your browser stores the images it receives. Therefore, the next time you visit the site, the browser doesn't have to download the images because they are already there on your hard disk. If an image in the site has been

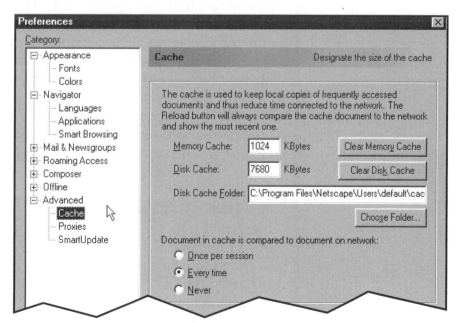

If you have trouble updating the images in your cache, clearing your browser's cache will erase all the temporary files your browser automatically stores to save download time when you surf the web. The examples above are from IE5 (top) and Netscape Navigator.

updated in between your visits, your browser may use the old version that is in the cache. Clearing the cache will erase all these images and force the browser to load fresh ones from the server. You clear the cache in Internet Explorer by selecting TOOLS/INTERNET OPTIONS from the main menu bar and, in the middle box (the one labelled "Temporary Internet Files"), clicking on the Delete Files button. In Netscape, select EDIT/PREFERENCES from the main menu bar, then ADVANCED and CACHE in the left window.

CHECKING FORMS

Checking forms involves two things: entering the information and verifying that the hidden fields are properly processed and that you get the information you entered back. You will, unfortunately, have to wait for your page to send the form to the CGI script, for the CGI script to process it, for it to post the result to your email address and then for this message to be made available to you by your ISP. This can take a few minutes, in the best of cases. While this is being done, start again and check the hidden fields: the NOBLANK, RECIPIENT and THANKSURL fields. If you get a message in your web browser saying that that the form couldn't be processed but are still receiving feedback from it via email, it means that you have made a mistake by entering a wrong parameter or value in the THANKSURL hidden field. The data is processed and sent to you, but when it comes to the last step – going to the "thank you" page – the process breaks down.

CHECKING EXTERNAL LINKS

Now that you have checked your site, you might have to check other people's. If you used external links in your pages, you have to make sure, first, that the site you point to is still there and, second, that the content of this site is still relevant to what you have in yours. Remember that you have no control whatsoever over what the external link is going to look like or be about. This issue is particularly important if you build a family site, or a kids' page: you don't want to link it to just about everything.

DESIGNING A SITE

There are simple rules to follow when designing a web page. The use of colours, shapes and text has to be carefully planned and, above all, coherent. A web site is a window to yourself or your company. If the design is messy, or technically faulty, it will reflect on you – badly. This chapter will give you an insight into designing a site that works and that is also informative, easy to use and entertaining.

COLOURS AND THE WEB

Knowing which colours to use in a web site is very important. Because a site will be seen on a multitude of different computers, each having a different monitor and in some cases a different colour palette, you should restrict yourself to using 256 colours.

256 colours doesn't seem to be a lot, but it is usually sufficient to convey the tone you want. These colours are usually called "web secure colours" and can be found in any major graphic design packages. They are called secure because they will not change with the configurations of your visitor's computer. 256-colour mode is the minimum people usually work with on computers. If you work in a higher colour mode, the 256 original colours will be contained in the larger palette. The number of colours displayed on a computer screen is called the "colour depth". To check the colour depth setup on your computer, right-click anywhere on your desktop, select Properties and then open the Settings tab.

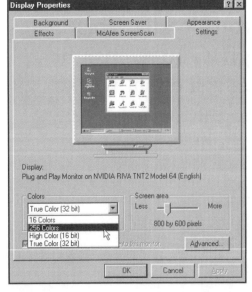

1 Check the colour depth in Windows Display Properties dialog box. You have a choice between 16, 256, thousands (called High Colour or 16-bit colour mode) or millions of colours (called True Colour or 32-bit colour mode). A colour palette shows all the colours available for each mode.

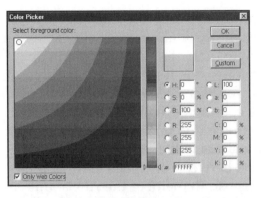

WORKING WITH 256 COLOURS

On the left is an example of two colour palettes: the 256-colour palette and the millions of colours one, as seen in Adobe PhotoShop. The reduced colour palette can seem like a hindrance, but it is usually enough for your purpose. Gradients and transparency effects will be the one to suffer the most, so try to avoid them if possible and use the JPEG format as explained on page 28 if you do use them.

2 As you can see, there are a lot of colours that won't be available to you when you work with only 256 colours. The millions of colours palette still contains the web secure colours and these are the ones you want to work with.

COLOUR SCHEMES

A colour scheme is a selection of colours that you will use in your site. These colours could be the ones appearing in your logo, for example, or the colours of your favourite football club if you choose to build a site in their honour. You should be aware that a heavy colour, such as a bright red or a deep purple, will be difficult to work with, because the other images in the page will still have to be visible on such a deep, colourful background and might have to be of high contrast to become so. Try to use a light colour for your background. Select <u>MODIFY/PAGE PROPERTIES</u> in the main menu bar and change the background colour from there.

BACKGROUND COLOUR AND BACKGROUND IMAGE

If your page has a background image, it is a good idea to set its background colour to a colour approaching the main one used by the image. If your image is, say, of a brown tone, choose a brown background colour. This way the page, when it starts loading in the web browser (before the background image is transferred), will first be uniformly brown and the transition between a blank background and a background image will be easier on the eye.

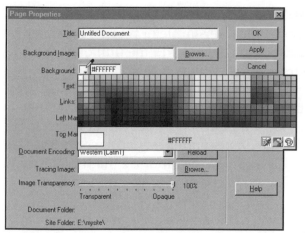

The colours you choose must be consistent throughout your site. To make the navigation of your site easier, you can colour-code it (that is, use a different colour for each section of a site), but even so the colour coding must be the same in all sections. If you do not follow this rule, your visitors will get confused and the relation between one page and another will be lost. Remember the rule about restricting the colour of hyperlinks that was described earlier.

1 Open the Page Properties Inspector and select a background colour from the colour palette by clicking on the square right of the Background label.

2 Place a Tracing Image via the Page Properties Inspector. Modify the opacity of this image by moving the slider left and right so that it doesn't interfere with the rest of the page's contents. Press Apply to see the changes made and then on OK when you are satisfied with the opacity level.

TRACING IMAGE

Dreamweaver 3 offers you the possibility of using a tracing image to help you place your web elements accurately in your page. The tracing image will not be visible in the web browser when you save your work but you will be able to see it as you work. This image must be in JPEG, GIF or PNG format. You place a tracing image in your page by selecting MODIFY/PROPERTIES in the main menu bar.

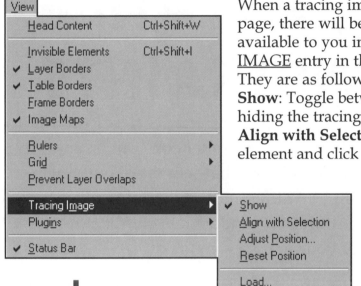

When a tracing image is placed in your page, there will be other options available to you in the <u>VIEW/TRACING IMAGE</u> entry in the main menu bar. They are as follows:

Show: Toggle between showing and hiding the tracing image.

Align with Selection: select a web element and click on this entry to align the top left corner of the tracing image with the top left corner of the object.

Adjust Position: set the tracing image position in the page in pixels.

3 Control the way the tracing image is displayed in your page with this menu.

Reset Position: this option will put the tracing image back to its original position, which is at the top left corner of the page.

Load: Use this option to load or change a tracing image. Once the tracing image is placed where you need it, move the layers containing your text and images to match it.

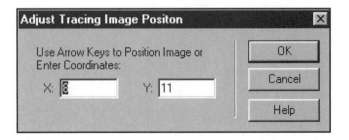

Enter the position of the tracing image in the <u>Adjust Tracing Image Position</u> dialog box. You can either enter specific numerical values or use the cursors keys to move the tracing image left or right, up and down by one pixel. If you press <u>Shift</u> as well, the tracing image will move in the specified direction by five pixels at a time.

SIZE, BALANCE, CONSTRAINTS

There are a few other constraints, apart from the use of 256 colours, that will make building a web page slightly different from building other types of multimedia product. One of them relates to the size of your graphics and text.

The Settings dialog box will show your current screen resolution. Move the slider to 800 by 600 to work in web design mode.

You saw the notion of colour depth in the previous section; that is the number of colours your screen can display. Now we come to screen resolution. The screen resolution is the amount of pixels per inch you display on your screen. When building a web site, it is customary to work with a screen resolution of 800 x 600 (which stands for 800 by 600 pixels per inch). So if you are fortunate enough to work on a big monitor, you might easily fall into the too-big-for-the-common-user error, which is to fill your page with images that your visitor might not be able to see without scrolling because they have a smaller monitor. To check your screen resolution, click anywhere on your Windows desktop and select Properties and then Settings.

800 by 600 is the screen resolution used by most people. That doesn't mean that everybody is going to use it. That doesn't mean to say that you are the only person on the planet with a big monitor. Unfortunately, it does mean that the images in your site might not be visible to your visitor because you can fit much more on your big monitor with a high resolution than they can. This size, 800 by 600, is a compromise.

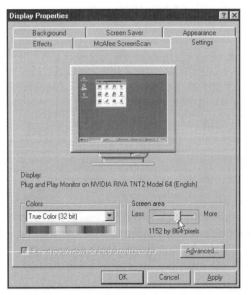

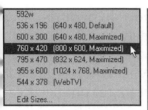

CHANGING THE SIZE OF YOUR WORK WINDOW

Dreamweaver lets you specify the size of your document window to reflect a particular screen resolution. To do this, look at the bottom of the document window and choose a resolution from the dropdown list. The dimensions given are those of the inside of a web browser when viewed in a given resolution.

1 Select a screen resolution to work with from the list. As you can see, the 800 x 600 size becomes 760 by 420. This is because the web browser will have a toolbar, a location bar and a menu that will take some room at the top of the screen.

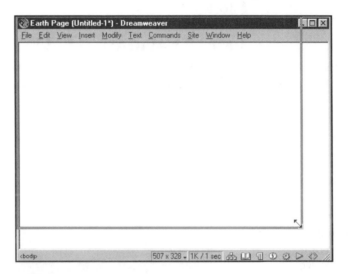

2 Each time you manually resize the document window by dragging the bottom right corner, its new size will be displayed at the bottom.

GRAPHICS AND SCREEN RESOLUTIONS

There is a great difference between viewing a page in a medium screen resolution and in a high one. Basically, a graphic that will look fine at 1024 by 768 will look inflated at a lower resolution. It will be huge. So how can you overcome this problem? The best way is to work in 800 x 600 to start with and make your graphic small enough for this resolution. Then check your site on a higher resolution and see if the graphics are still readable. If your image contains text for instance, make sure that this text is roughly the same size as the common font size in your web page. As for other graphics, simply try to make them small. The visitor with a bigger monitor will be used to seeing smaller graphics, anyway.

When you bring up new windows from your hyperlinks, keep this screen resolution in mind. It is extremely easy to build a page on a big monitor and then forget to check the result at a lower resolution. If you did not tell the web browser to display a scrollbar in the new window (which you might not need when working in a high resolution), some information will be lost.

MAKE NAVIGATING EASY

Information must be easily accessible at all times. Frames are ideal to provide a map for your site and to access all sections of a site at the click of a button. Don't let this prevent you from adding a line of text links at the bottom of each page, though. This way your visitor doesn't have to go to the frame to navigate when they have finished reading a page: the links are at their disposal straight away.

Duplicate the menu that was in the frame at the bottom of the pages themselves: navigation will be even easier. Use a small font for this line of hyperlinks.

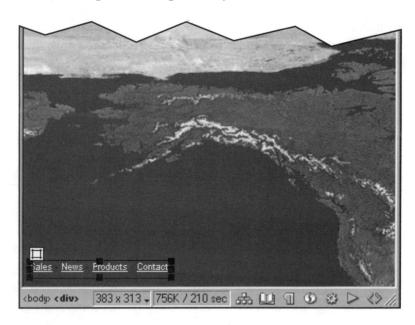

In the same vein, when you use anchors, always add a "Back to the top" or a duplicate of the anchors' menu links. If you don't, your visitor will have to scroll all the way up, which is tedious – and you don't want your web site to be tedious.

CLARITY OF CONTENT

Another simple rule to follow is to make sure that the information, once accessed, is clear and understandable. Do not put a hundred images where a couple would suffice. Space out your images so that they can be easily related to the accompanying text. On the other hand, do not be too minimalist, either. A page with a collection of symbols for links might not be as clear as you think, although they may be very nicely designed. A beautiful graphic that nobody understands will look good but will be totally ineffective unless you provide a clue as to what it means.

These buttons look great, but without the explanations underneath them they would be useless on a web page.

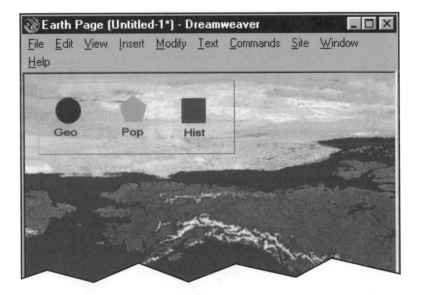

Your site must be consistent. If you choose a logo, a shape or a gimmick, repeat it across your site. Always have the name of your site visible somewhere on each page. It needn't be outrageous publicity, just a single line or a small graphic present everywhere. If you can link this to your homepage (the first page your visitor will be taken to when opening the site, usually a "Welcome to" page), it is even better. Don't put too much information on a single page; build another one instead and link the two. Find a balance between entertainment, readability and impact.

USING A FLASH ANIMATION

HTML is not the only way to build a web site. There are other packages available on the market that will produce stunning sites with a minimum of HTML coding in them.

The best known alternative web site design package is certainly Macromedia Flash, a cross between a web site-building program and an animation program. In its fourth version, Flash is the tool preferred by many a webmaster. With a bit of practice and training, Flash can transform the way you look at web site-building.

Brian Dister
Gary Grossman
Slavik Lozben
Jared Kaplan
Murat Konar
Peter Santangeli
Robert Tatsumi

macromedia® FLASH™ 4

macromedia®

Quality Assurance:
team   thanks   legal

Version 4.0 • © 1996, 1997, 1998 , 1999 Macromedia, Inc.
All rights reserved. Macromedia, the Macromedia logo,
and Flash are registered trademarks of Macromedia, Inc.

MACROMEDIA FLASH 4

Flash 4, unlike Dreamweaver and other web design packages, will not produce HTML code. It works in a totally different way by enabling you to use graphics and animating them to create surprisingly small files viewable by all web browsers.

When building a Flash animation, you start with a blank document. To this you add objects which you can modify (rotate, resize, alter, skew, colour them, etc). These object can then be animated, using a multitude of options, and they can also be assigned hyperlinks. Each object can be assigned a state matching the behaviour of the mouse for finely-tuned interactivity.

A Flash animation (movie) is seamlessly integrated into your HTML page.

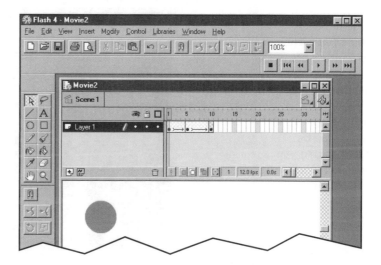

As illustrated in the following pictures, the objects in flash can be modified and animated extremely easily.

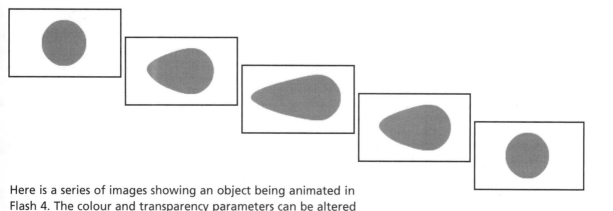

Here is a series of images showing an object being animated in Flash 4. The colour and transparency parameters can be altered during the animation too.

There are two big advantages to working with Flash. One is the extraordinary amount of control you have over your animations. The second is that a full page, with plenty of links, text and animations, will still be very small and be downloaded in seconds. The only drawback is that you have to use a plugin to view these pages, although recent browsers have one included in their installation process.

This page has been built using Flash. The rollover buttons are a breeze to set up and will be much smaller in file size than conventional rollovers. Each image can be assigned a link, so you don't need to worry about HTML anymore.

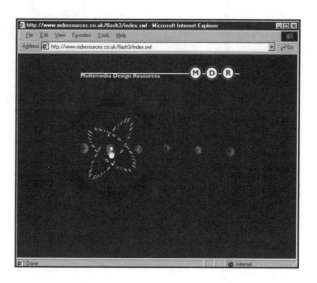

Flash can handle hyperlinks and forms, so you can build a site in Flash from beginning to end. It can also deal with the MP3 music file format. You can also build your site the conventional way and pepper it with small Flash elements. If you use Flash for your whole site, you have the added bonus of being able to make an executable file out of a Flash movie: build your site with Flash and then save the result as a Windows or a Macintosh program. Because it will be very small in size, you can include a button somewhere in your site to offer your visitor the possibility to download the whole site and view it offline when they are not connected. All they need to do is to double-click on the program – as for any Windows or Macintosh program – and your site is launched on their computer, without them having to pass through a web browser.

1 Click on <u>Flash</u> in the <u>Objects</u> menu.

INSERTING A FLASH MOVIE

Dreamweaver has a dedicated button for adding Flash movies in the <u>Objects</u> palette. A Flash movie is a page or a series of pages that has been created in Flash. To insert one, first create a layer for your movie and click on the <u>Insert Flash</u> icon to choose the file to work with.

2 Your Flash movie inserted in a Dreamweaver web page will look like a grey rectangle with the Flash logo in it.

Now that your Flash file is inserted, have a look at the <u>Flash Properties Inspector</u> for a range of options. If you cannot see all the options, click on the down arrow on the bottom right corner to expand the <u>Properties Inspector</u>. The most useful basic functions are explained on the next page.

3 Set the various options for your movies in the <u>Flash Properties Inspector</u>.

A MOVIE ON YOUR PAGE

Flash is not an HTML editor. It is more a movie-making program than anything else. It has timelines, scenes and frames, and a Flash file is called a movie.

Green arrow: click on this arrow to run the Flash movie while designing your page in Dreamweaver. The arrow will change into a red square on which you will have to click to stop the preview.

W/H: if you need to modify the size of the movie, enter the new values (width/height) here. Unlike an image, the sharpness of the movie will not be altered. It is better to leave the dimensions as those of the original file, though.

Quality: this determines the quality of the animation in your page. As with everything on the web, the higher the quality, the longer the movie will take to load.

Loop/Autoplay: use these radio buttons to have the Flash movie loop and run as soon as it is loaded. If you do not check the Autoplay button, you will need to trigger the animation by assigning an Action to it from the Behaviors palette.

CONTROLLING A FLASH MOVIE

First select the image that will trigger the action (i.e. playing the movie) and press F8 to bring up the Behaviors Inspector. Click on the ± symbol and select Control Shockwave or Flash.

1 Select the Control Shockwave or Flash entry in the dropdown menu that appears when you click on the ± symbol in the Behaviors tab.

2 Check the various radio buttons to decide what will happen when the image is clicked on. If you have more than one Flash movie in your page, select the one you want to work with in the <u>Movie</u> list.

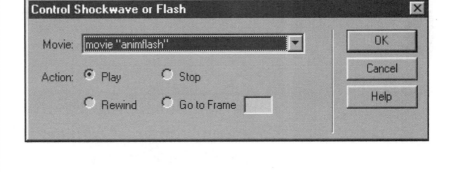

Macromedia Flash is unique in its field. If you master it and integrate your movies in your site, you will be able to create stunning pages. For more information relevant to the actual workings of Flash, refer to the manual.

VRML

VRML (Virtual Reality Modelling Language) is another way to make your sites more interesting. It will create 3D sites but is a lot more complicated than Flash for animating and navigating.

Have a link to a VRML world in your page and enjoy 3D chat in a wide variety of environments.

PLUGINS

Plugins are small programs that will register with your web browser and will enable you to open special file formats that you might encounter on the web. They represent a valuable complement of your site and their usefulness shouldn't be overlooked.

RealPlayer is a plugin that will open its own window to run the files it deals with.

Some file formats have been specifically developed – or modified – for the web. These format were designed to make your sites even more interactive and attractive. These plugins come in two forms: ones that will run in a new window and ones that will open the specified file on the original web page. Plugins are free and available online from the homepage of the company that produces them. Plugins are usually designed to bring new media to your site: video, music, VRML, audio streams etc. Some plugins will already be present on your system, depending on the version of the web browser you use. Some you will have to go and get at the source. In any case, you have to make sure that your visitor knows that you are going to use a file format that will require a plugin to be viewed properly.

WHY DO I NEED A PLUGIN?

Plugins will enable you to use movie clips, music, animation, virtual reality and plenty of other things. Plan your site in detail and think whether or not you need to integrate such information into your site. If you do, read ahead and check which plugin is the one you need; then refer to the address section of this book to get them.

Macromedia Flash: as you learned in the previous section, Flash pages will only be visible with a plugin. In fact, a Flash movie in a page comes with special options to fetch the plugin it needs automatically.

Macromedia Flash comes with its own plugin detection facility.

RealAudio:this one deals with music. An audio stream loads in your computer memory and is played continuously. QuickTime: distributed by Apple, this plugin is used primarily to play movie clips that have been made on a Macintosh. It is available for Windows and Macintosh and can also run other movie files.

WinZip is a handy plugin that works with compressed files.

WinZip: WinZip is a compression program. The latest version can decompress archive files straight from the web.

This list is not exhaustive. Each time you work with a program that requires a plugin to use the files it generates on the web, you will find detailed instructions and addresses in the manual. This should be on the manufacturer's web site.

WARN THE VISITOR

It is good form to let your visitor know that to view a page, they will need to get a plugin. Generally, their web browser will detect the presence of a file and will warn them to get the plugin for it. A small graphic is enough to tell them beforehand. If you use Flash, for instance, it is advisable to create two sites – one with and one without Flash animations – and give your visitor a choice between the two.

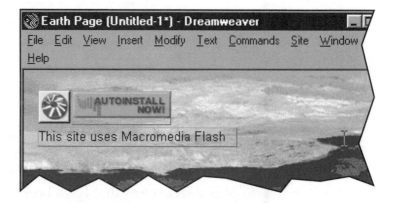

Warn your visitor that they need a plugin to view a particular page. Be good to them, though, and show them how to get it.

THE DRAWBACK OF PLUGINS

There is one problem with plugins, which is that they require the authorization of your visitor to install. Some people, when they work on a network, cannot install new software on their machine. Some people will also be distrustful of anything requiring an external program or won't bother waiting a few minutes for the plugin to install.

INSERTING A PLUGIN OBJECT IN DREAMWEAVER

Dreamweaver has a special button for inserting plugins in your page. It is in the <u>Objects</u> palette.

Once the plugin object is placed on your page, check the <u>Plugin Properties Inspector</u> and enter some details. The most important information needs to be typed in the <u>Plg URL</u> field. This needs to contain the URL of the page from which your visitor will be able to download the plugin if it is not already installed on their system. Get this address from the people who distribute the plugin. Dreamweaver can detect the presence of some well-known plugins when the page is loaded and redirect the visitor to a new page according to whether the plugin is or is not available. To use this feature, click anywhere in your page and press <u>F8</u> to view the <u>Behaviors</u> tab. Click on the ± symbol and select <u>Check Plugin</u>.

1 Click on a layer to place a plugin into, and then on the <u>Insert Plugin</u> icon in the <u>Objects</u> palette.

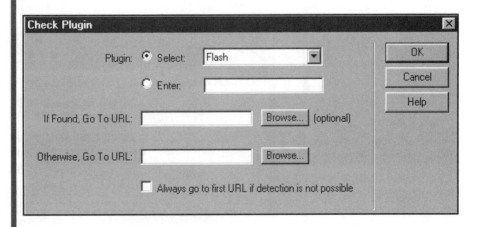

2 Use the <u>Check Plugin</u> dialog box to decide what to do if a plugin is found present or lacking. Select the plugin you want Dreamweaver to detect automatically from the list. Use the <u>If Found...</u> fields to give URLs of the pages you need your visitor to go to in case the plugin is found, or where to go if the plugin is not found.

MAKE YOURSELF KNOWN

Publishing a site on the web is only the beginning. In order for people to come and see it, they must know that it exists. With millions of pages available online, yours could easily pass unseen.

In order to be known, you have to register your site with search engines. A search engine is a special site whose aim is to search the web for sites matching the visitors' search criteria. Search engines will browse through a database of sites that have been registered with them, so if your site is not part of this database, you won't appear as the answer to someone's search query.

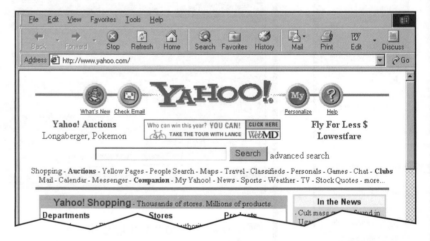

Yahoo.com is one of the best-known search engines. It has the added bonus of being able to search its categories. A search string (also known as a query) is entered in the empty box and all you have to do is press the <u>Search</u> button to display a list of relevant sites.

REGISTERING YOUR SITE

As explained page 166, search engines work with a database of site addresses that have been registered with them. The process has been made easier and faster, but it can still take a while (a few days) for your site to be registered. The best way to go about this is to go to a search engine homepage and look for a "Register new site" hyperlink.

Another very well known search engine: www.lycos.com. Nearly all the search engines have a button to register new sites somewhere on their homepage. Registering is quick, easy – and usually free!

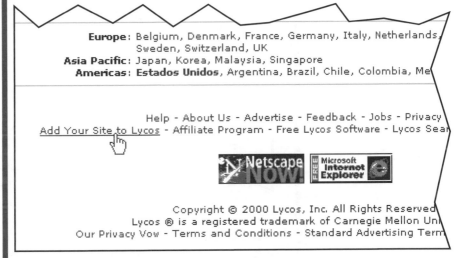

The main information you need to enter will be the complete URL of your site. A complete URL means absolutely everything, including the www. part, the domain name part and also the exact name of the file that is your homepage. If you have followed this book carefully, you will have named your homepage index.html. This is fine for a browser, because it will recognize index.html as being the file in your site to open first; therefore you can give your address to people as being www.mycompany.com and not www.mycompany.com/index.html. A search engine doesn't work this way and you need to enter www.mycompany.com/index.html. You may even have to type http:// before the address. Check the FAQ (Frequently Asked Questions) page of the search engine or follow the onscreen instructions .

Enter the full URL of your site (its complete web address) in the Enter your URL box. Do not miss out any of the address or your site will be wrongly registered.

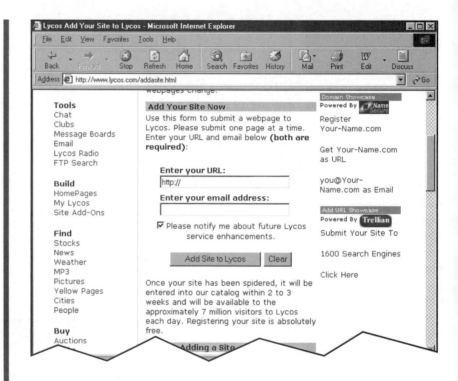

SPIDERING

Spidering is the process followed by the search engine to register your site. It consists of going to your site, checking the URL, checking the meta tags, (contents and keywords, explained earlier) and adding it to their database of sites. It may take a few days for this spidering process to complete. So wait, come back to this search engine and type a query relative to your site, for example its title. When the spidering is done, your site will appear in the list along with any other sites relevant to your query.

REGISTER IT

http://register-it.netscape.com/ is a search engine-registering site. From within one site, you will be able to register with 12 search engines for free. This way, you will not have to visit each search engine one at a time to register your site. There are other sites that offer this service, but you will find that you have to pay for most of them.

Register It is a site that will take a lot of the hassle out of registering.

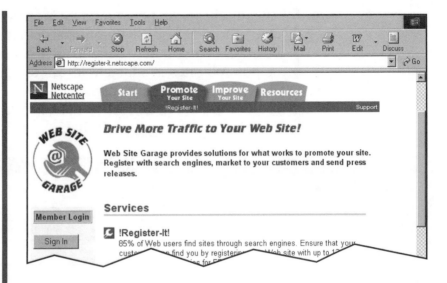

Go2Net's Metacrawler is a very popular meta search engine.

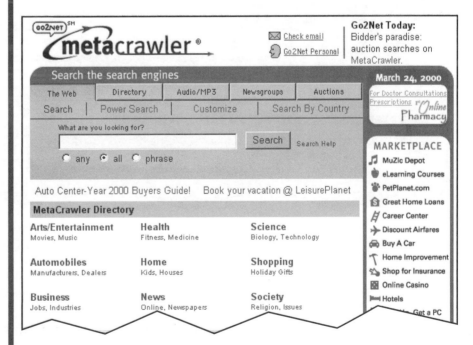

META SEARCH ENGINES

A meta search engine is a search engine that will search other search engines. Instead of looking for your query in their own database, they will contact those of the main search engines instead. These can help you a lot because some sites might have been registered with one particular search engine but not the others, so you may have to switch search engines to get all the possible sites available relevant to your query. Type a query in a meta search engine and it will bring you back results from the databases at Yahoo, AltaVista, Lycos etc., without you having to visit them.

The web is full of sites offering banner exchange programs.

BANNERS

While you were viewing a web site, you may have come across a banner advertising another site. When you click on the banner, you are taken to the site in question. This is common practice and can help you with getting visitors to your site if you don't mind having a banner on all of your pages. The principle is simple: you build a graphic advertising your site, submit it to a large banner exchange organization that will place it at random on other sites registered with them and in exchange you agree to have a banner or two advertising another site on yours.

The banner exchange organization will provide you with all the necessary details as to how to build your own banner and how to host someone else's. It is just a matter of copying some code into your page and it is very easy to do. This is perfect for small, hobby-type pages. If your site is a commercial one, you might be better off relying on other forms of advertising as you don't have any control over what will appear in this banner on your site. You might display a banner from a competitor, which wouldn't look good at all.

You must also consider whether or not the presence of a banner may disturb the coherence of your site. Banners are usually narrow rectangles and could clash with the overall design of the page. Also, as you have no control over which banners are displayed, you might have to display banners advertising something you do not agree with.

LINKING TO PROFESSIONAL SITES

It may happen that you want to include links to professional sites in your own site; for example, to provide your visitor with an opportunity to learn more about a given topic or to send them to a company whose product is relevant to the content of your site. This shouldn't cause any problem in most cases, but you must be aware that not all companies will be happy to have a link from your site to their. Big companies have whole departments dealing with marketing and company profile and your site might not fit their idea or image. It is always a good idea to ask permission before using someone else's logo or other information. You could end up in a whole lot of trouble if you do not (after all, material on the web is copyrighted).

The inverse situation might even happen: that your site is so nice, so successful that big companies are interested in providing you with a link to their site for publicity reasons. This could happen if your site is about children or children's books: it is not unrealistic to imagine that a publisher might come and ask you to build a link to their site. If this happens, use your negotiation skills and ask for something in return.

READY-MADE SCRIPTS

On the web you will find numerous tools to spice up your pages such as counters, guest books, cookies etc. They come in the form of small scripts and bits of code that you can easily integrate into your HTML.

Once you are confident about your web site-building skills, there is no reason why you should not experiment a bit further and add functionality to your site with the help of small JAVAScript codes which you can get free from a variety of sites across the web. Some scripts will need the help of your ISP to implement but other are just a matter of opening the HTML editor to see the inside of your page and adding a small piece of code.

The HTML Source icon

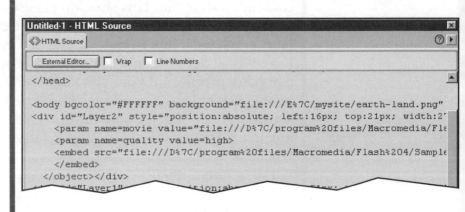

1 See what your page is made of by opening the <u>HTML Source</u> tab. Press <u>F10</u>, or select <u>WINDOW/HTML SOURCE</u> from the main menu, or click on the <u>HTML Source</u> icon in the launcher.

Here is an example of a script you might find on the web. This will make your text hyperlink change colour when passed over.

```
<HTML>
<HEAD>
<TITLE>My Page</TITLE>
<STYLE>
A {color:blue}
a:hover {color:red}
a:visited {color:lime}
a:active {color:purple}
</STYLE>
</HEAD>
<BODY>
<BR>
</BODY>
</HTML>
```

And here is the HTML code for a blank document in Dreamweaver 3:

```
<html>
<head>
<title>Untitled Document</title>
<meta http-equiv="Content-Type" content="text/html;
charset=iso-8859-1">
</head>
<body bgcolor="#FFFFFF">
</body>
</html>
```

There isn't a great deal of difference in size, is there? All you have to do is copy the lines that are different in the first code and paste them exactly as they are at the matching place in the Dreamweaver code. In this case, everything from </TITLE> to </STYLE> has to be copied and placed just after </title> in the second code. Now type some text in a layer in your actual page and assign an hyperlink to it. All the text hyperlinks you will make for this page will change colour from blue to red when the mouse passes over them. That wasn't too difficult, was it?

TAMPERING WITH HTML

As you just saw, modifying your HTML code isn't too difficult. It can be a delicate operation to perform at times but it is relatively safe. The best way to go about it is to do a broad search for "free scripts" in any search engine and pick a site in the resulting list. There are heaps of sites ready to give you free scripts and all will have detailed instructions as to how to set them up. The code on offer will not mess up your pages, as long as you follow the instructions carefully. Here is another very useful bit of code that will redirect your visitor to another page after a given amount of time. This is an example of the type of instruction you might get with a free script:

Make an index.html or index.htm page in the folder containinga meta tag in the HEAD section as below.
The five stands for redirect after five seconds. Please do not make this below five.

```
<HTML>
<HEAD>
<meta http-equiv="Refresh"
  content="5;URL=http://www.mycompany.com">
</HEAD>
<BODY BGCOLOR=WHITE>
</BODY>
</HTML>
```

All you have to do is paste this section into your HTML and change the amount of time, and then add the address of the page you will be going to (currently www.mycompany.com).
   If you read through the meta mag section of this book, you will be able to do this quite easily. If you didn't, here is how to

do it. First, select <u>INSERT/HEAD/META</u> from the main menu bar. The <u>Insert Meta</u> dialog box appears. In the <u>Attribute</u> list, select <u>http-equivalent.</u> In the <u>Value</u> field type "Refresh". In the content box, type "5;URL=www.mycompany.com". That's it. After an interval of five seconds, the viewer will be taken to the page <u>www.mycompany.com</u>. Modify the interval in seconds and the URL to redirect to according to your needs.

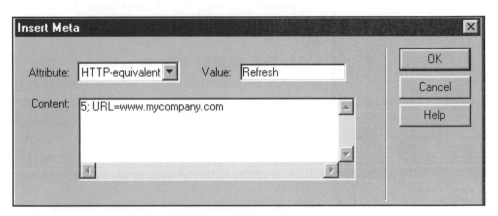

Insert a meta tag in your page and follow the instructions. You could also have copied the relevant code and pasted it into your HTML.

COUNTERS

Page counters are useful to keep track of the traffic on your site. Every time someone lands on your site, their visit increases a counter by one. Counters can be very different from one another in the way they look, but they all work in the same way. Most of the time, counters are set up by your ISP. You will therefore need to contact them to get more information as to how to add one to your site.

You are user number **1 3 4 9 7 9** to access this page since 9 December 1997.

Check how many visitors you get in a day (your hit rate) with a counter placed on your homepage.

Web counters usually work with CGI scripts, so you will have to rely on your ISP for support. ISPs usually have a web counter feature in their package. There are also numerous sites offering you free page counters if you sign up with them and accept a little publicity for their services on your pages. As for banners (see page 170), it all depends on the type of site you are building. Counters can be modified to match the design of the pages they appear in and they do not have to start at number 1 if you don't want to look unpopular.

SIGN THE GUEST BOOK

Another plus you can add to your site is a guest book, which is basically a feature to enable visitors to view and leave messages and comments. Shop around for the "Free Guest Book" button you will undoubtedly encounter on your journeys through the web. You will be taken to a site that will set everything up for you free.

A guest book can be a great way to get feedback from your visitors and to create a kind of online community.

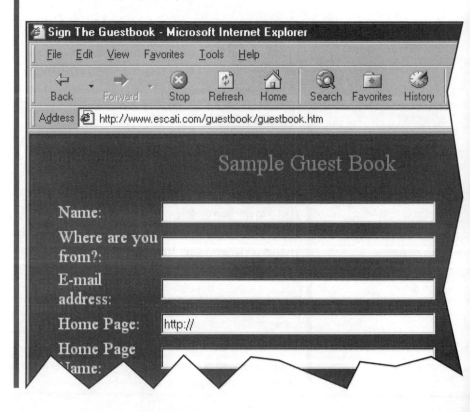

COOKIES

No, installing a cookie on a computer doesn't mean putting a biscuit in the CD tray. A cookie is a very small file that is installed by some sites and that contains some information about you (well, your computer). These cookies are harmless and will not disclose anything you don't want to be known. They are often used to check whether you have visited the site before. If you haven't, you will be taken to a welcome page, and if you have, the page will say, for instance: "Glad to see you again on our site". This nifty little program is very easy to use and to set up; simply go to a free script site and follow the instructions. Cookies will store information for a certain amount of time and then be erased. You can turn off the cookie option in your web browser if you don't want any to be installed on your computer.

A WHOLE WORLD OF SCRIPTS

More accurately, a World Wide Web of scripts. It is impossible to list and show examples of all the scripts and coding you can get your hands on from the web – there are simply too many of them. Look and you'll find hundreds.

Free web space providers such as GeoCities will often not let you use scripts. Make sure you know what you will be getting from your ISP.

EXPLORER AND NAVIGATOR

Released by Microsoft and Netscape respectively, these are the two main browsers presently available on the market. Your visitor will most probably use one of them.

The first thing to realise is the fact that not all browsers behave in the same way. They are said to be standard (indeed HTML is the standard in web page format), but some browsers will recognize certain commands while others won't. The way frames are displayed in IE5 is not the same as in Netscape – there is a few pixels' difference. So if you have created the perfect frameset, be aware that it might look awful on a browser other than the one you checked it with. These are the joys of web site design… Fortunately, web design programs know all about web browsers' quirks and will help you overcome them.

Always check your work in both major browsers, Internet Explorer and Netscape. You will notice that your framesets will not look the same from one browser to the other.

WILL IT WORK?

Dreamweaver enables you to check how your page will behave in more than one browser. Select <u>FILE/CHECK TARGET BROWSERS...</u> in the main menu bar and choose how a particular browser will display your site. This option is mainly used to check a page in an old browser and see what are the elements that will cause problems.

1 The <u>Check Target Browsers</u> dialog box. Select a browser from the list and press <u>Check</u>.

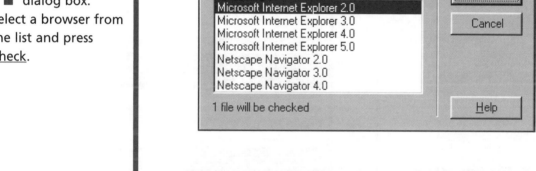

2 Here is what you want to see: no errors whatsoever in your file, which will be displayed perfectly, in this example, by Internet Explorer 2.

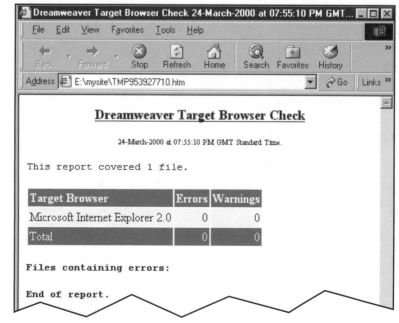

3

Errors, if there are any, will be listed and explained for each check.

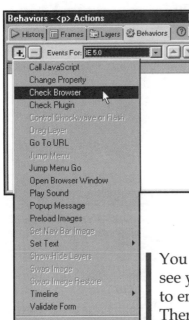

You don't know which browser your visitor is going to use to see your site. If they use an old browser, they will not be able to enjoy fully the pages you have carefully laid out for them. There is no way you can build a site for each browser from Microsoft IE2 or Netscape Navigator 2, though. It's just too much work. The thing to do in this case is to create a few special introductory pages. Let Dreamweaver check the browser your visitor is running and redirect them to the page specially created for it. This page could simply be a warning (to inform the user that they are missing out on some features of your site) or a link to download the latest browser. To build in a browser check, press F8 to bring up the Behaviors tab. Press the ± symbol and select Check Browser from the list. This will launch the Check Browser dialog box.

1

Select Check Browser in the list.

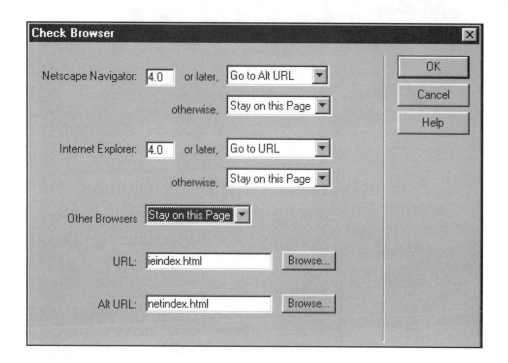

2 Use this dialog box to redirect your visitor to a given page according to the browser they use. Click on the down arrow next to <u>Other Browsers</u> to select what to do in case the browser your visitor is using isn't listed in the Netscape Navigator or Internet Explorer boxes, or in case they use an older version.

If you are using frames in your sites and you are really worried about perfection, you will have to build at least two pages; one for IE and one for Netscape, and change the frame dimensions slightly in order for the frames to display correctly. As a frame is loaded only once, all the other pages can be shared by both browsers. You might also want to make sure Macintosh users will view your site correctly: a page created on a Windows system will look different when viewed on a Macintosh system. There are many scripts available on the web to detect the platform your visitor uses and redirect them to the appropriate pages. In this case, you may have to do a new version of your site with a smaller font.

GLOSSARY

Translation is a difficult process, but all it takes is practice. Here are a few key words an phrases that you may have missed during the course of this book.

ACTION
An Action, in Dreamweaver, is something that happens because an Event has taken place. The Event could be clicking on an image, for example, and the Action could be a new hyperlink opening up in a new browser window.

ANCHOR
A hyperlink that points to a certain position in a page.

CGI SCRIPTS
Small programs hosted by your ISP that will perform a variety of actions, usually send you back a form via email. CGI scripts are usually written in programming languages, C++ or PERL, for example.

CONTEXTUAL MENU
The dropdown menu that appears when you right-click on your page or an element in your page. For the AppleMac user, these menus can sometimes be accessed by Ctrl-clicking.

COOKIE
A small file left on your hard drive when you visit certain sites on the Internet.

DIRECTORY

A directory is the same as a folder. It can also mean the path to this folder as in "C:/my folder".

DOMAIN NAME

This is the "dot com" part name of your URL, as in www.mybrand.com. When you sign up with an ISP, you get your ISP's domain name. To get your own, you must register a name with a company that specializes in such dealings. Domain names can end with just some of the following suffixes: .net, .org, .co.uk, .com.uk, .fr, .ie and so on. The number of possibilites is expanding very quickly.

DRAG AND DROP

To drag and drop is to click on an object or a file in a folder, hold the mouse button down and release the button only when you have moved the object or the file where you wanted it to go.

EVENT

An Event is a state of the mouse, of the keyboard, of the Timeline or the page itself. An Event, in Dreamweaver, can trigger an Action (such as the event onMouseOver [when the mouse moves over an image] can trigger a rollover).

FLASH

A program, made by Macromedia, that creates animations to display (mainly) on web pages. Many people use these animations instead of (or more commonly as well as) HTML. The The only drawback of Flash is that it requires a plugin.

FORM

A form is a request for information online. It is made of form elements such as text fields, check boxes and radio button, etc. The form, when submitted, is usually sent to a CGI script (stored on a remote server) that sends you back the content of the form via email.

FRAME
A page can be divided up into frames, each of them containing another web page. When many frames are incorporated into a single page, the page is called a frameset. Each of the frames can change to display a new page independently of the other frames on the page.

FTP
File Transfer Protocol. This is the file transfer method used to move files from your computer to your remote site.

GIF
An image file format. GIF files are particularly useful on the web because they are very small.

HTML
HyperText Markup Language. The language used by web browsers to read web pages – and the language web design programs use to create these pages. HTML is made up of instructions called tags.

HYPERLINK
Also known as a link, it is an instruction to jump from one page to another, or to a file. You can have links to other files on your site (internal links) or links to other sites on the Internet (external links).

IMAGE MAP
An image that is divided up into separate areas, each of which act as hyperlinks. When your mouse passes over an image map, the cursor will usually change to indicate that there are links available.

INDEX.HTML
The page which is going to be opened first by your visitor's web browser. It is usually your welcome page (homepage).

INTERNET CACHE
A special folder in which web browsers store pictures of the web pages you visit, so that next time you go to the site, they are already available on your hard disk (thereby cutting down the time spent downloading them).

IP ADDRESS
An Internet Pathway address is a set of numbers assigned to any computer when connected to a network. When you type www.mycompany.com in the location bar of a web browser, you tell the browser to look for the computer with the IP address matching the domain name.

INTRANET
A company's own internal network, available to a limited number of people only, unlike the Internet. An intranet usually looks and behaves just like the Internet, however.

ISP
Internet Service Provider – the people who provide you with a connection to the web.

JAVASCRIPT
A more powerful language than HTML, used to perform more complex actions such as rollovers, menus and lists.

JPEG
An image file format which uses a variable rate of compression, allowing you to an amount of say in the file size-quality trade off.

LAYER
A layer is a box in which you place elements such as images, text, buttons and so on. Layers can usually be moved around as you create your web pages.

LEASED LINE
A permanent connection to the internet.

META TAGS

Meta tags are used primarily to insert keywords and comments for search engines to display and therefore for people to look up your site with.

PLUGIN

A small piece of software that a web browser needs to be able to see certain objects that it encounters on the Web. Plugins are usually available for nothing but your download time.

PNG

A relatively new image file format for the Internet.

REMOTE COMPUTER

The remote computer is the one you are connected to on a network. The one you work on at home or at work is called the local computer.

ROOT DIRECTORY

Your root directory is the folder that contains all the files (and all the folders inside it) needed by your site. If your site wants a file (such as an image) that is not stored in the root directory, the file will not be displayed in your browser.

SEARCH ENGINE

These are sites you go to when you want to search for a site on the web. They are also the sites you go to when you want to make your own site available to a search by other Web surfers by registering with them.

TARGET

The target is the name of a frame that a hyperlink points to, when you are linking to a frameset.

TERMINAL WINDOW

The windows that pops up when you have successfully connected to an FTP site.

TEXT FIELD

A element in a form that enables your visitor to enter some text. This text will be sent back to you via email when your form is processed.

THUMBNAILS

A small version of a bigger image, often linked to its bigger counterpart so when it is clicked on, the larger file opens up in a new window.

UPLOADING

Transferring a file from your local computer to a remote computer, usually via FTP. The opposite operation is called downloading.

URL

Uniform Resource Locator. This is a web address (www.something.com). In other words, a unique file on the internet that you point your browser to.

WEIGHT

The weight of an image is its file size in kilobytes.

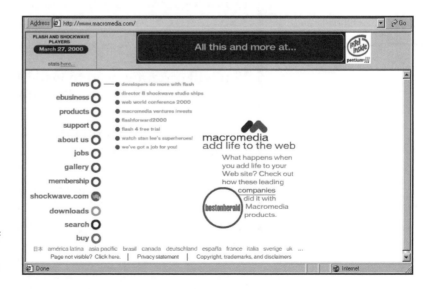

Flash plugins and trial software are just a few of the goodies available on the macromedia Web site

WEB ADDRESSES

If you need anything to build your site, you might as well go and get it at the source, the web itself. There you will find resources such as images, backgrounds, CGI scripts, JavaScript code, demonstration version of popular software, etc. Browse this mine of information and grab all you can.

The first place to go could very well be the Macromedia homepage at www.macromedia.com, as you will find downloadable demonstrations of Dreamweaver, Flash, Fireworks and a host of other application specialized in design in general and web design in particular. This site uses Flash technology and will offer you a wealth of information and showcases.

WEB BROWSERS
You will certainly need to visit Microsoft and Netscape homepages, as they too offer information of web techniques. You can download the latest versions of web browsers from there as well as updating the one installed on your machine, whatever the platform you use (Windows or Macintosh). Microsoft site is pretty big, so be prepared to use the extensive search facilities to get the information you need. Netscape homepage is called "Netcenter" and is at www.netscape.com. www.microsoft.com: a giant site containing links to multiple download pages.

SEARCH ENGINES

Search engines are the place to go to surf the web in search of information. Whatever you need, query it from a search engine and you will get dozens of addresses linking to sites you might find interesting. The best known search engines are www.yahoo.com, www.altavista.com, www.lycos.com, www.infoseek.com and www.excite.com. These are not the only ones, far from it. The web is literally crawling with search engines, and speaking of crawling, you might try www.metacrawler.com, a meta search engine, and so is www.1blink.com.

WEB HOSTING AND ISPS

It is impossible to give a list of all the free web hosting sites available on the web. www.homestead.com, www.geocities.com, www.bizland.com, www.tripod.com, www.homepage.com… These free sites are often "grabby", which means that they will ask for a contribution on your pages such as the insertion of a banner or a logo with a link to their site. All of them offer free web space, free email, often also free web design and things like counters and guest book. As to ISP, your best bet is to check a computer magazine and check the addresses of free and paying ISPs from there.

CGI, JAVA. JAVASCRIPT AND HTML SOURCE CODES

The easiest way to go about that is to do a search for "free CGI scripts" in any search engine. You will get hundreds of links back from your query and be able to choose exactly what site matches your level of expertise. www.javascript.com offers JavaScript of the cut and paste kind (that is you cut the code in the example and paste it into your HTML source and Bob's your uncle). The site is clear and offers links to other JavaScript related information. www.cgi.resourceindex.com is a list of links to CGI scripting related sites. Most of these sites have links to tens of other sites and contain information about HTML, SHTML. DHTML etc.

INDEX